INTRAPRENEURING IN ACTION

Intrapreneuring
in *Action*

· ·

A Handbook
for Business Innovation

GIFFORD PINCHOT
& RON PELLMAN

Berrett-Koehler Publishers, Inc.
San Francisco

Berrett-Koehler Publishers, Inc.
235 Montgomery Street, Suite 650
San Francisco, CA 94104-2916
Tel: (415) 288-0260   Fax: (415) 362-2512   www.bkconnection.com

Ordering Information

Quantity sales. Special discounts are available on quantity purchases by corporations, associations, and others. For details, contact the "Special Sales Department" at the Berrett-Koehler address above.

Individual sales. Berrett-Koehler publications are available through most bookstores. They can also be ordered direct from Berrett-Koehler:
Tel: (800) 929-2929; Fax: (802) 864-7626; www.bkconnection.com

Orders for college textbook/course adoption use. Please contact Berrett-Koehler:
Tel: (800) 929-2929; Fax: (802) 864-7626.

Orders by U.S. trade bookstores and wholesalers. Please contact Ingram Publisher Services, Tel: (800) 509-4887; Fax: (800) 838-1149; E-mail: customer.service@ingrampublisher services.com; or visit www.ingrampublisherservices.com/Ordering for details about electronic ordering.

Printed in the United States of America

Library of Congress Cataloging-in-Publication Data
Pinchot, Gifford.
     Intrapreneuring in action : a handbook for business innovation / Gifford Pinchot & Ron Pellman.
       p. cm.
     Includes bibliographical references and index.
     ISBN 1-57675-061-2 (alk. paper)
     1. Industrial management.   2. Creative ability in business.
    3. Organizational effectiveness.   I. Pellman, Ron, 1940–   II. Title.
HD31 .P497 1999
658.4'063--dc21   99-047667

First Edition
15 14 13 12   10 9 8 7 6

Interior Design: Gopa Design   Proofreading: Elinor Lindheimer
Editing: Stanley Marcus   Indexing: Paula C. Durbin-Westby
Production: Linda Jupiter, Jupiter Productions

To Don who started us in the innovation business,
to Lennart, Gustaf and Sven who did much to make
intrapreneuring a worldwide phenomenon
and to intrapreneurs and sponsors everywhere.

We wish you well.

Table of Contents

PART FOUR:
THE CLIMATE FOR INNOVATION

APPENDICES

PREFACE

THIS IS A BOOK about practical ways to achieve more effective innovation. It is for anyone involved in any way with innovation and change in business—which is to say, essentially every employed person, from CEO to shop-floor worker.

Why aim at such a broad audience? Our goal is to help all players in the innovation game understand how to be effective. To play his or her position well, each player has to understand the viewpoints and responsibilities of the other players. Whatever your level within your organization, we hope to make innovation more fun, more profitable, and better aligned with your deepest values.

Understanding innovation in large organizations begins with understanding the role of the intrapreneur. *Intrapreneur* is short for *intra*-corporate entre*preneur*. Within an organization, intrapreneurs take new ideas and turn them into profitable new realities. Without empowered intrapreneurs, organizations don't innovate. Yet many organizations waste their intrapreneurial talent. Too often one of us will receive a Sunday evening phone call from a troubled intrapreneur wrestling with concerns about what he or she will face at work the next morning. These calls rarely involve technical or marketplace issues. Almost invariably, the concern relates to some perceived internal threat to the person's project, team, or career.

In some cases the fears are overblown, but too often the threat is real. Management is blocking legitimate intrapreneurial zeal with bureaucratic quibbling or industrial-age "We know best" attitudes. In the worst instances, a single individual resists an initiative for change because his or her own domain may lose power or influence. What bothers us is the frustration, waste of resources, lost opportunity, and quenching of the human spirit that result from the failure to apply the fundamental principles of innovation management. We hope our book will help individuals and organizations avoid such needless waste.

Learning to innovate more efficiently and effectively is a little like learning to lose weight. The basic rules are simple, and they work, but it is a struggle to follow them. In both cases, discipline, commitment, and courage are essential.

The following chapters present both "bottom-up" and "top-down" perspectives on the struggle to achieve world-class rates of innovation. They offer no easy fixes and no promises of overnight success. Instead, they are loaded with well-tested fundamental principles and detailed guidance on implementation.

We know from firsthand experience that these principles work. We have helped more than five hundred intrapreneurial teams launch their innovations and have witnessed their varying degrees of success. We've worked with teams that took ventures from a raw idea to sales exceeding a billion dollars. We've assisted in launching new businesses, new products, new services, cost-reduction initiatives, and enterprises whose customers were other parts of the same company. We have seen good tries that might have made it but for the impact of unforeseen events. And we have seen sad failures that resulted from neglect of the basics of effective intrapreneuring. This book is a summary of what these experiences have taught us.

HOW TO FIND
WHAT YOU NEED IN THIS BOOK

Though this book is designed to be read from beginning to end, you need not follow that pattern. Rather than starting at Chapter 1, you can use the following chapter summaries to choose where to begin.

PART ONE:
THE BASICS OF INTRAPRENEURING

Part One sweeps away the myths often told about innovation and covers the basics of what you will need if you are going to manage innovation effectively.

CHAPTER 1: HOW INNOVATION ACTUALLY HAPPENS

Innovation never happens according to plan. This means that in innovation it does not work to expect intrapreneurs to achieve the results laid out in the business plan. Good intrapreneurs are like broken field runners: they change the plan on the fly as new information appears. How then does one manage innovative projects? Read on—the answer emerges from a single secret!

CHAPTER 2: THE CRUCIAL ROLES IN INNOVATION

The key to managing innovation is understanding the five distinct roles in the innovation process as it actually happens. The five roles are (1) idea generator or inventor, (2) intrapreneur, (3) intrapreneurial team member, (4) sponsor, (5) innovation climate maker. Manage them well and you will have success. Leave out any role and innovation slows to a crawl.

CHAPTER 3: HOW TO SUCCEED AS AN INTRAPRENEUR

This chapter focuses on the intrapreneurial actions and attitudes that lead to intrapreneurial success. Never lose sight of the six imperatives described here and your chances of success will be very good.

CHAPTER 4: WHAT AN INTRAPRENEURING PROGRAM LOOKS LIKE

This chapter shows how to align the intrapreneurial energy of your organization around key challenges and how to support intrapreneurs in meeting those challenges. It covers tools such as the innovation fair and just-in-time intrapreneurial training.

Some fear that intrapreneurs are born, not made, and that therefore intrapreneurial training is a waste. It turns out that training can both bring out the intrapreneurial spirit hidden within and give intrapreneurs the tools they need to succeed. It can also strengthen the intrapreneurial team and move an idea from concept to business plan. But it must not be theoretical. Intrapreneurs learn by doing, so give them the right sequence of challenges and just-in-time hints on how to meet them. Intrapreneurs learn quickly when doing so helps them move toward implementing their idea. This chapter shows you how to train intrapreneurs.

PART TWO:
FROM IDEA TO PROFITABLE REALITY

Part Two guides the intrapreneur through the process of turning an idea into a profitable reality.

CHAPTER 5: FINDING A GOOD IDEA

This chapter begins with the core of creativity: how to come up with ideas until you feel secure in the knowledge that you have too many good ones. Then you can comfortably reject those that don't fit who you are or where your company needs to go.

How, then, do you choose which ideas to pursue? Learn the surprising answers. Quickly sort through hundreds of ideas to find the ones that can lead you to a meaningful success. This chapter applies both to choosing ideas for yourself and knowing when to invest in the ideas others bring you.

CHAPTER 6: GETTING STARTED

You have chosen a new idea and want to get going. What are your first steps? What should you avoid? The chapter includes tips on communicating your idea, an outline of the intrapreneurial financial model, and three key questions to ask as you roll into action.

CHAPTER 7: AVOIDING TYPICAL NEW PRODUCT MISTAKES

This nuts-and-bolts chapter takes you through the most common new product mistakes and shows you how to avoid each one:

1. Market misunderstanding
2. The missing intrapreneur
3. Strategic misalignment
4. Slow execution

CHAPTER 8: INTRAPRENEURING WITHIN A STRUCTURED DEVELOPMENT PROCESS

In all probability, your company has adopted a structured innovation development process that does as much to get in the way of innovation as it does to encourage it. Don't worry. Your competitors face this sort of thing, too. This chapter has numerous hints on how to fine-tune a structured process and how to add the flexibility that makes it effective.

PART THREE: THE TRICKS OF THE TRADE

Part Three contains the distilled lessons of our fifteen years of coaching intrapreneurs and their managers.

CHAPTER 9: ADVICE FOR HANDS-ON INNOVATORS

This chapter is a distillation of the tricks of the trade for working intrapreneurs and their teams. It identifies the twelve essential behaviors that differentiate the successful intrapreneur from the "good soldier." Be sure you understand.

CHAPTER 10: WHAT YOU CAN DO AS A MIDDLE MANAGER

Innovation won't happen without middle managers sponsoring and protecting it. While many of the old information-collecting and packaging jobs of middle management are being taken over by computers, these innovation responsibilities are increasing. Learn to be an effective sponsor of innovation.

CHAPTER 11: WHAT YOU CAN DO IN SENIOR LEADERSHIP

We are assuming that you want to create a fast-moving, innovative organization that takes the world by storm. This chapter shows you how.

PART FOUR:
THE CLIMATE FOR INNOVATION

Part Four gives you the tools to diagnose and improve the climate for innovation in your organization.

CHAPTER 12: DIAGNOSING YOUR CLIMATE FOR INNOVATION

1. What are the key success factors that make an organization effective in innovation?
2. How does your organization score on these factors?
3. How can you build a climate that gives you faster, more strategic, and more cost-effective innovation?

You can find the answers to these questions by using the Innovation Climate Questionnaire in this chapter. Also visit www.pinchot.com for downloadable and on-line versions of the questionnaire.

CHAPTER 13: IMPROVING YOUR CLIMATE FOR INNOVATION

Once you have diagnosed your climate for innovation, this chapter shows you how to find the right prescription for improving it.

CHAPTER 14: THE FUTURE
OF THE INTRAPRENEURIAL ORGANIZATION

As organizations become more intrapreneurial, the basic principles of organization, management, and order evolve. Where are we going? This chapter reveals the organizing principles of the post-bureaucratic organization.

Introduction: The Principles of Effective Innovation

RAPID AND COST-EFFECTIVE innovation is the primary source of lasting competitive advantage in the twenty-first century. Other sources of competitive advantage are only temporary. Brands endure only if constant innovation in both product and marketing keeps them fresh. Low cost positions are soon lost without innovation. Control of channels of distribution is valuable only as long as customers prefer what they find in those channels. Technological dominance obviously rests on innovation. Even de facto standards like the Windows® operating system would be replaced by something better if not supported by energetic innovation. In the twenty-first century, we are left with no choice but to innovate well or to cease to exist.

Intrapreneuring in Action is about a better way to make innovation happen inside established organizations. Innovation is more than creativity. It is the creation and *bringing into widespread use* of a new product, service, process, or system—from the first glimmer of an idea to successful implementation and exploitation. Coming up with good ideas is generally not the bottleneck in the process of innovation. The real challenge is turning those ideas into profitable realities—a job that requires employees to behave like entrepreneurs.

The principles we present here apply to all kinds of innovation, including:

- New products and services
- Better ways of reaching customers
- Techniques for doing more with less
- Quality improvements
- Cycle-time reductions
- Novel methods of lessening environmental impact
- Improved organizational systems and structures
- New approaches for gathering and distributing information

1

■ Better internal services
■ New forms of employee and stakeholder participation
■ Anything else that makes the world or the organization a better place

INTRAPRENEURSHIP EVERYWHERE

Wherever we find innovation in large organizations we find intrapreneurs making it happen. Every innovation, large or small, requires some courage, some vision, and a willingness to take charge and make it happen. The tireless persistence and practical imagination of the intrapreneur are essential to the success of any new idea.

Even the little everyday innovations that keep a company responsive to customers begin with a vision of how to serve customers better or more cost-effectively. They grow out of a small dream and require significant initiative and courage to carry through. Even the most minor innovation thus represents a small intrapreneurial act.

Intrapreneurs naturally arise because they are passionate about making some idea a commercial reality. But though intrapreneuring is almost everywhere, so are management practices that make it more difficult. In this book, we will show how to radically increase the rate of innovation—without increasing the financial resources devoted to it. We will show how to bring out, focus, and guide the organization's intrapreneurial energy without frustrating its intrapreneurs.

THE INTRAPRENEURIAL TEAM

Few intrapreneurs today are soloists. Most work in intrapreneurial teams. The best teams are cross-functional or cross-disciplinary, bringing together several quite different viewpoints and professions in the service of a common cause. Each team member devotes himself or herself to creating and implementing a shared vision. Most teams are led by one intrapreneur, but all the members of the team can be called intrapreneurs as long as each understands the whole dream and is continually working to find better ways to make it happen.

When we meet with intrapreneurial teams, it is often difficult at first to tell who is from which function. Technical types make marketing suggestions and marketing types help solve production problems. In the early stages of an innovation, sharing all major issues with the whole team helps to create an integrated vision and to make sure that no issue "falls between the chairs."

THE SPONSOR

No intrapreneurial team could long survive without the services of a sponsor, a person of some clout who coaches, protects, and marshals resources for the team. Sponsors provide "air cover" and suggest strategies for winning allies rather than making enemies. With a good sponsor, the team can focus on making the innovation work rather than on approvals and internal politics.

Every successful team generally has several sponsors. As the team's initiative evolves, new sponsors are needed to release new kinds of resources or levels of spending. New functions, businesses, and geographies become involved, and the team reaches out for sponsors who can help it in those new areas. By the later stages of the project, the team will have built a coalition of active sponsors helping it succeed.

THE "INTRAPRISE"

In talking about intrapreneuring, you will find that you need a general word for the entity the intrapreneurs are creating. In intrapreneuring we often talk about the *venture,* but this does not exactly fit a process breakthrough or a service to other parts of the organization. *Enterprise* is more general than *venture* and captures the sense of creating both a bold result and an ongoing organization or team. We use the modified word *intraprise* (an enterprise inside the company) to denote what intrapreneurs are creating, whether the end result is a new product, new service, new process, or new venture.

A successful intraprise will usually develop a life of its own, garnering the enthusiasm not only of its founders but of new team members and customers as well.

COST-EFFECTIVE INNOVATION IN LARGE ORGANIZATIONS

Large organizations face special challenges in innovation. Unless they make good use of the intrapreneurial energy of their people, cost-effective innovation won't happen. "Good use" means, in part, that intrapreneurs are given considerable freedom to act. Too often we observe frustrated intrapreneurs waiting for permission to act and seeing their best ideas rejected. This is a waste of intrapreneurial potential and dooms the company to discouraging results and downsizing. However, freedom is not the whole answer. Good use of intrapreneurial energy requires that it be directed toward what is most important. How can we integrate the two apparently conflicting demands of freedom and organizational focus?

As we shall see, coordination, direction, and freedom can be combined in a practical way that predictably gets outstanding results. What? Predictability in innovation? Is it possible?

Violating certain principles of intrapreneuring can almost guarantee failure. If you want to see predictable failure, try appointing a team to an intrapreneurial job when the members don't believe in the idea. If you want widespread failure of innovation in your organization, punish those managers who stand up for intrapreneurs. Or try discouraging people who "waste resources" by helping out innovators in other parts of the organization.

Adhering to the principles of effective innovation does not guarantee the success of individual ventures. Innovation goes beyond what we can now see, and thus risks running into a dead end. But following the principles of cost-effective innovation will greatly increase the probability of success. It will reduce cycle time, increase the return on investments of time, energy, and resources, and reduce the cost of failures. Here are a few of the principles that will help clear your path as an intrapreneur.

THE PRINCIPLES OF COST-EFFECTIVE INNOVATION

MAKE YOUR MISTAKES FASTER AND CHEAPER

Innovation in the bureaucratic style takes nearly forever and uses a mountain of resources to achieve mediocre results. Expensive studies delay actions that could lead to more rapid and cost-effective learning. Intrapreneurial innovation finds a quicker, less expensive way to try out an idea, get feedback, and evolve toward a better offering. In general, the time for big spending is after a successful pattern has been demonstrated on a small scale. Then quickly ramp up investment to grab market share and stay ahead of the competition.

In the beginning, use rapid prototyping and seek early customer involvement. Get the innovation out fast and then continually improve it on the basis of customer feedback. Open your channels wide so that you learn rapidly.

BET ON PEOPLE, NOT JUST IDEAS

Many traditional management practices are based on making sure subordinates get the results specified in the plan. However, since innovation never goes according to plan, betting on *plans* for innovation is foolish. When making investments in innovation, bet instead on a team of people who can fix things fast when they don't work as expected.

RECOGNIZE REAL INTRAPRENEURS

Your ROI (return on investment) from innovation will rise steeply if you know how to tell real intrapreneurs from "promoters." Promoters identify and sell the objective but don't have the inclination or practical skills to roll up their sleeves and work on achieving it. They seek to innovate primarily as a route to advancement. Real intrapreneurs find intrinsic value in the visions they pursue. They will often deliver good results even if their original plan proves wrong. (See Chapter 10, page 90 table: Differences Between Real Intrapreneurs and Promoters.)

DON'T FILTER OUT THE TRUTH

Innovation is about learning what works and what doesn't. If you filter the truth, learning will slow to a crawl. Don't allow bureaucrats to sanitize the facts. Build open systems that distribute learnings from both successes and failures without labeling people in the process.

TREAT THE TEAM AS A SINGLE ENTITY

The team is a unit, collectively responsible for the success or failure of the whole. Reward the whole team, not just the leader or some member judged to be outstanding. Future cooperation depends on it.

DON'T TRIGGER THE CORPORATE IMMUNE SYSTEM WITH GRANDIOSITY

Promote early-stage ideas modestly, lest you scare people into opposing you. Inside the company, share your initial concept with friends first. They will give you the feedback you need to correct obvious flaws without broadcasting your idea to its natural enemies. Talk with potential customers as much as possible, but focus on learning, not on telling people how great your idea is.

VALUE ALL KINDS OF INNOVATION

A better process may be just as important as a better product. Improving service to internal customers may liberate the energy of many others. A system that allows a company to learn faster, to think better, or to care more about customers may change its fate. Honor all kinds of innovation; all are necessary to build a great organization.

CHOOSE INNOVATIONS THAT FIT WHO YOU ARE

There are many potential customers and many things each of those customers might need. You can't do them all. Look for ideas that will matter to customers, build on the company's strengths, and fit with your own values and talents. If an idea makes good sense intellectually but doesn't grab your heart, don't commit to it. Intrapreneuring demands whole-person commitment. If your heart is not there, let someone else do it. You won't find the energy to carry you through the dark nights that every innovation hits along the way to success.

LIVE WITH YOUR CUSTOMERS

No one can adequately describe to you how your customers think, so don't just hire market researchers—experience customers yourself. Go beyond interviews and focus groups. Learn about your customers' needs by watching them, noting their problems, and then (oh, heresy!) figuring out what you would want in their situation. Spend time with them until they say, "You sound just like one of us." Now you are in a position to go beyond what they say they want to what they will demand once they see it. Only an intimate understanding of customers is a reliable guide to innovation.

BUILD FINANCIAL MODELS EARLY, BUT DON'T BELIEVE ANY OF THEM

Intrapreneurs have to "do numbers." Spend time thinking about the steps to success in numerical terms. How many customers do you need? How many employees will it take to serve them? What do all the parts of your vision cost? To answer these questions, you have to do detailed imagining, but that is what a clear vision consists of. In the beginning, make up some numbers. These are called SWAGs—Scientific Wild-Assed Guesses. Even SWAGs will reveal critical issues and sharpen your thinking. Then do the research necessary to get a bit more reality into your plan.

SPONSORS, PRACTICE LOWERING YOUR STATUS

Though sponsors must have the position and clout to keep the corporate immune system from destroying intrapreneurs, that very rank and power may also intimidate the intended beneficiaries. Awe may lead intrapreneurs to make major mistakes if they take their sponsor's offhand suggestions as commands or if they keep the sponsor in the dark about unpleasant truths. To guard against such disasters, sponsors must move closer to a peer relationship with the teams they are sponsoring. If you are a sponsor, learn to spend time with the team without taking over. To do this, find ways to lower your status while with the team. Begin by literally lowering yourself. Sit down and, if need be, slouch until your head is lower than theirs. Standing tall is a hardwired biological signal of dominance. Practice being less scary, and as a result you will hear what is really on the intrapreneurs' minds.

REACH OUT ACROSS BOUNDARIES

Most innovation requires working together across the boundaries of the organization. For this reason, organizations whose culture and systems support cooperation across boundaries are more innovative. Learn how to cross boundaries without making waves. Thank those in other areas who help you or help your people. Support others who come into your area for help. Don't tolerate "turfy" (turf-protecting) behavior.

BUILD ORGANIZATIONAL COMMUNITY BY HONORING GENEROSITY

The heart of community is the pleasure we take in doing for others without asking for anything in return. Innovation is such a gift; it creates the future for everyone in the organization. Learn how to build generosity across organizational boundaries and thereby raise the capacity to innovate manyfold.

Let innovators, like a sports team, be a symbol for the success of the whole company. Since credit is not a limited resource, create more of it by taking the time to celebrate innovation and success. As in a movie, make sure everyone who helps ends up on the list of credits. The more you can make innovation a game in which everyone wins, the more people will support innovation in all the everyday decisions that are beyond your control.

PART ONE

THE BASICS OF INTRAPRENEURING

CHAPTER 1

HOW INNOVATION ACTUALLY HAPPENS

Every organization—not just business—
needs one core competence: innovation.
                    —Peter F. Drucker[1]

THERE IS A GROWING URGENCY to innovation these days. Innovation is necessary to differentiate one's offering, to find and fill unoccupied spaces in the market, and to keep up with the soaring productivity of competitors. One has to innovate faster and faster just to stay in place.

With innovation playing an ever larger role in business success, organizations are striving to find ways to get more effective innovation per dollar. This is not surprising. As we move into the information age, the proportion of any organization's budget devoted to innovation is growing rapidly. Getting your money's worth from innovation efforts has therefore become the hallmark of effective leadership.

Leaders just starting out in the innovation-boosting business often focus most of their energy on creativity. Of course, more and better ideas contribute to innovation, but the big gap in the innovation process is the capacity of the system to implement ideas rapidly and cost-effectively. Implementation requires intrapreneurs to transform the conceptual into the actual. In many organizations there is a shortage of working intrapreneurs, and potential innovations languish in the space between conception and commercialization. The shortage of intrapreneurs is not the result of poor hiring; it is caused either by a lack of sponsors to protect and encourage intrapreneurs or systems that make life so tough for sponsors and intrapreneurs alike that few dare to come out of their holes to innovate.

The basics of effective innovation are (1) providing a focusing vision that guides the intrapreneurial energy of the organization; and (2) liberating the intrapreneurs to achieve that vision. Focusing and releasing the intrapreneurial spirit of even a part of a company can result in a flood of innovation. Consider the rebirth of Fleischmann's.

INTRAPRENEURING AT FLEISCHMANN'S

The Fleischmann's Company, part of Nabisco, consisted of only three brands in two mature markets: Fleischmann's and Blue Bonnet margarines and Egg Beaters, a liquid egg product. Without new products, the company's prospects for significant growth were grim.

To break out of humdrum performance, the company first established a strategic intent—to create innovative products for the refrigerated section of the supermarket, with a special focus on healthier eating. They then encouraged their would-be intrapreneurs to find ways to create and launch those products.

As ideas fitting the vision emerged, Fleischmann's management supported many of them, allowing the intrapreneurial new product teams to act without waiting for the normal multilevel approval process. In just one year, Fleischmann's' intrapreneurs developed and commercialized four highly successful new products:

- SnackWell's Chocolate Nonfat Yogurts
- Fat Free Squeeze, used in place of margarine
- A fat-free squeezable cheddar product
- Easy Omelets, a two-minute microwave omelet

As Jim Goldman, director of marketing, put it, "A key to this success was a broad-based awareness of the importance of these initiatives, a real empowerment across functional groups, and a willingness to commit to breakthrough results without having all the action steps buttoned up and specified in advance."

MAKING YOUR MISTAKES FASTER

Many organizations have difficulty managing innovation because they insist on an orderly world in which results turn out exactly as planned. This doesn't work because innovation requires the exploration of unknown territory. Success in innovation depends not on the certainty of being right, but on rapid learning and fast response to what has been learned.

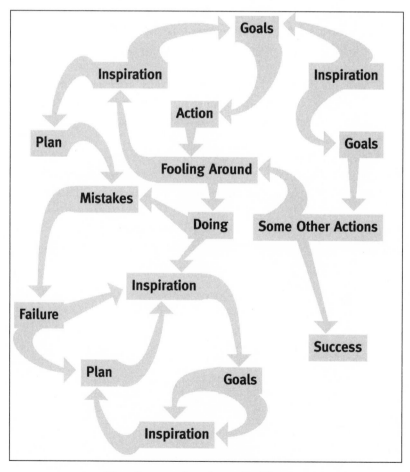

How Innovation Actually Happens

The fact that real innovations don't occur according to plan is a challenge to traditional styles of management. How can we manage innovation effectively if we cannot trust plans when moving into unknown territory?

A clue: Venture capitalists say,

I'd rather have a class A entrepreneur with a class B idea than
a class A idea with a class B entrepreneur.

Picking the people with a passion for making the idea work is more important than picking the right plan. The plan will be proven wrong within a short time as the team makes mistakes and learns from them. But if you have picked a good team and given them freedom and accountability, it will most likely find a way to make something worthwhile happen. Perhaps this is the reason why venture capitalists say they base 80 percent of the decision to invest on the quality of the people in a venture team and only 20 percent on what those people plan to do.

Corporations can greatly increase their return on innovation efforts by moving the emphasis in their innovation management systems from selecting the right plan to selecting the right team to trust. This is a fundamental shift. Bureaucracy is based on the idea that people are essentially interchangeable parts. But intrapreneurs are not interchangeable and cannot easily be replaced.

CHAPTER 2

THE CRUCIAL ROLES
IN INNOVATION

I NNOVATION PROCEEDS BEST when each of five key roles is performed well. This chapter describes those roles and how they work together.

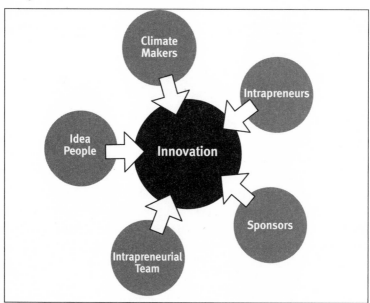

The Crucial Roles in Innovation

IDEA PEOPLE

Everyone is capable of creativity. In some the talent is buried—trained out by schools, parents, or bosses. In the information age, part of every manager's and every team member's job is to create an environment in which creativity is appreciated and new ideas are brought out of everyone, even those who may have forgotten their capacity to be creative. However, ideas are like insects: many are born, but few live to maturity. There are far more good ideas than can ever be implemented. Part of growing up is to realize that nearly every good idea you have is doomed to die without ever being tried. For this reason, good ideas alone are not enough. To move forward, good ideas must capture the enthusiasm and commitment of an intrapreneur.

INTRAPRENEURS

Because they closely resemble entrepreneurs, we call the people who turn ideas into realities inside an organization "intrapreneurs." The intrapreneur may or may not be the person who first comes up with an idea. Intrapreneurs roll up their sleeves and get things done. They recruit others to help. Whether working on an idea that was originally their own or building on someone else's, they are "the dreamers who do."

INTRAPRENEURING AT TEXAS INSTRUMENTS

Texas Instruments is well known for intrapreneurial successes like the digital signal processing (DSP) chip business, which is the main source of profit for the company today; Speak and Spell, the educational toy; FLIR (Forward Looking Infra Red), which allows pilots and fire fighters to see in the dark, chips to decompress MP3 Internet audio; and calculators. The company studied fifty of its successful and unsuccessful new product efforts. In each of the successes there was at least one dedicated intrapreneur who persisted despite great obstacles. Conversely, the common denominator of the failures was the absence of a zealous volunteer champion. Innovations just don't happen unless someone takes on the intrapreneurial role.

Most people face a choice: either go to their graves with all their better ideas unfulfilled, or give up on 99 percent of them and take the time to push one at a time through to completion. Once you focus on making one specific idea happen, you become an intrapreneur.

THE INTRAPRENEURIAL TEAM

The ideal intrapreneurial team consists of volunteers, generally recruited to the idea by an original intrapreneur. They form a core group that stays with the project from its early stages to well past its initial commercialization or implementation.

3M'S PROJECT SYSTEM

In the renowned 3M project system, an idea would be brought forward by a team of three: one person from marketing, one from research, and one from manufacturing. The commitment of the three members meant that the venture had already passed through three different screens, so management gave it the benefit of the doubt. And why not? Three good people with very different functional viewpoints had each decided they were willing to invest a significant part of their careers developing the idea. Getting the personal commitment of a professional from each of these three functions is a tougher test than most management reviews.

Furthermore, the existence of the self-forming team points to the presence of an intrapreneurial leader who has recruited the others without a lot of support from above. This kind of team has more resilience than one appointed by remote leaders. In the 3M project system, this core team ideally stays together until the project has grown into a full division.

Thus, very early in its history, 3M developed a system for betting on a team rather than just management's evaluation of an idea. This fundamental shift helps to explain 3M's long history of innovation success.

Unfortunately, because of the analytical sophistication of 3M's current management systems and the growing size of its divisions, the tendency of the original intrapreneurs to stay with the business they have formed after it has become a division has declined. Will the lack of this part of the innovation system affect the motivation of 3M's intrapreneurs? Only time will tell.

The quality of a team arises not just from the attributes of its individual members; the way those members relate to each other is equally important. How well do they understand each other's strengths and weaknesses? How well do they work together to capitalize on the strengths and overcome the weaknesses?

GENERAL DORIOT SELECTS A TEAM

General Georges Doriot, who was a professor at Harvard Business School, is often called the founder of the venture capital industry because his investments in start-ups were so successful that other investors followed his lead. Here is some insight into how he selected his investments.

When a team initially came to see him, the first thing he did was to "knock them flat." No matter how good the idea appeared to be, he told them it was no good. Then he watched to see how quickly they picked themselves up off the floor and came back at him. This he saw as a test of their courage and persistence, essential qualities for successful entrepreneurs (and intrapreneurs). His second test was less obvious. After watching them for several meetings, he asked himself, "Are they laughing?" If the answer was yes, they passed. But why was laughter so important? Doriot explained that what he was looking for was not a collection of individuals with great résumés but rather a team that had learned to work together. If they had been through the team-forming process, they would know each other well enough to make fun of and with each other, but if they hadn't, they would still be treating each other too carefully to kid around. Unless he saw strong relationships within the team, he did not invest.

We have seen terrific ideas coupled with good people run aground simply because the teamwork failed. In many of these cases, the team did not form through self-selection and recruiting; rather, people were assigned a leader and told what to do. Intrapreneuring is tough enough that most such teams fail.

When building intrapreneurial teams, select volunteers who are well accepted by the other members. Make sure that the leader is someone the team members respect, know, and want to follow. If the team is not there yet, keep investment modest and the membership open to change. If an appointed leader doesn't rapidly earn the team's respect, let the members choose a new leader.

THE SPONSOR

Sponsors support their people's ideas by protecting them from the "corporate immune system." They coach intrapreneurs, raising tough questions and then letting the intrapreneurs find their own answers. They help the group garner needed resources. More specifically, effective sponsors:

1. *Create a compelling vision that calls for and focuses innovation efforts,* thereby pulling potential intrapreneurs with compatible ideas out of the woodwork. A good vision stretches the organization beyond what it can accomplish without substantial innovation. It gives a clear direction so that the ideas that come forward are aligned and together achieve critical mass. It indicates how the organization's assets can be used to win a far more favorable position than would be possible under business as usual.

2. *Bet on people, not just ideas or plans.* Good sponsors look for a strong intrapreneurial team that is eager to implement before they invest significant resources or trade in valuable political chips.

3. *Take the time to coach and guide the intrapreneurial team.* In order to be able to share ideas and make comments without appearing to take over, they have to learn to lower their status so as to become "one of the team."

4. *Anticipate political obstacles and block oncoming tacklers.* This involves both behind-the-scenes lobbying and helping teams avoid potential hornets' nests.

5. *Provide resources themselves or coax resources and permissions out of others.* A good sponsor has to help others understand the importance of the venture so they will want to support it, too. In the end, a good sponsor gives credit to others for the role they have played in developing the intraprise.

We have studied hundreds of innovations within large organizations. In every case, at least one sponsor guided the intrapreneurial team around obstacles and intervened with the hierarchy to keep the project alive. Just as there is no innovation without persistent intrapreneurs, and no significant innovation without intrapreneurial teams, there is no innovation in large organizations without courageous sponsors.

THE CLIMATE MAKER

When the Hewlett-Packard corporate climate began to favor committees over the entrepreneurial spirit, the founders came out of retirement to reaffirm the company's commitment to intrapreneurship. They didn't intervene in any specific project, as a sponsor would. Rather, they worked to create an organizational pattern and culture in which businesses had intrapreneurial freedom and effective sponsors could empower many successful intrapreneurial teams. Growth and profitability, which were beginning to stall, took off again.

In the complex world of today's multinationals, it takes more than one or two climate makers to create an environment that brings forth sponsors and intrapreneurs. It takes a widely shared belief in innovation and a sincere determination to keep it alive. See Chapter 12 to find out what kind of climate-making your organization needs most.

CHAPTER 3

HOW TO SUCCEED
AS AN INTRAPRENEUR

OVER THE YEARS we have asked successful intrapreneurs for the secret of their success. Most give credit to the team, but there are a number of other important factors that we have identified by "listening between the lines."

DAYDREAM IN DETAIL

Successful intrapreneurs are thinking and dreaming about their ventures most of the time. They often get their best ideas while driving the car or taking a shower. They daydream about ways to move their ideas forward and visualize how they will deal with potential obstacles. They play out possible mistakes in their imagination, thereby minimizing the risk that they will make those mistakes in reality. By imagining options, they find hidden opportunities. Such thinking is both an obsession and a key to intrapreneurial success.

If you are not drawn to doing this sort of detailed imaginative work, it may be a sign that your idea does not grab you at a deep level. Ask yourself, "Is it really aligned with my values? Do I really believe it can work? Why am I not in love with this idea?" Don't commit to an intrapreneurial idea unless it has a firm grip on your imagination.

DO ANY JOB NEEDED TO MAKE YOUR IDEA A REALITY

According to the bureaucratic theory of organization, when everyone does his or her specialized job as directed by the boss, the whole works together to create value for the customer and the shareholders. In a classic bureaucracy, workers are told, "Don't think. Just screw in these two bolts as the engine passes by on the assembly line. Everyone else will do their little job, and the boss will make sure that a car comes out at the end of the line." Perhaps this sort of hierarchical coordination once worked well enough. Today, it is increasingly unworkable.

The world is changing so fast that we all need to continually check that what we are doing integrates well with the work of others to produce value for the customer. In any case, for intrapreneurs, a system that does "everything else" so that they can concentrate on one special job doesn't exist. Intrapreneurs are the self-appointed general managers of a new idea. Every aspect of moving the idea forward is their responsibility. If something needs to be done, they must either figure out how to get someone else to do it or do it themselves.

When they become intrapreneurs, engineers often have to do market research, and market researchers have to go to the law library. As Howard Head said of the founding of the Head Ski Company, "When the floor needed sweeping, I swept the floor. When the sales force needed a rousing speech, I gave a rousing speech." Like other successful entrepreneurs, he did whatever needed to be done.

Don't let the fact that you are not qualified stop you from doing something that needs to be done. Robert L. Schwartz of the Tarrytown School for Entrepreneurs liked to quote G. K. Chesterton: "If a thing is worth doing, it's worth doing badly." He did not mean that quality should be abandoned but that in the process of blundering your way to success, it is far better to do a job as an amateur than not to do it at all.

ASK FOR FORGIVENESS, NOT PERMISSION . . .

Besides striking, one way British labor unions put pressure on employers is by "working to rule." When labor follows every rule to the letter, manufacturing plants slow to a crawl. If "working to rule" can play such havoc with relatively well-defined and predictable manufacturing processes, imagine what it can do to a chaotic process like innovation. For this reason, the innovator must have the courage to do what needs to be done, even if that means bending or ignoring the less important rules. If you take this approach and anyone objects, ask for forgiveness—then keep going. But you may be surprised how infrequently anyone does object!

. . . BUT RESPECT THE WATERLINE

Of course, as with every other rule, one can go too far in not asking for permission. The trick is to know when to "just do it" and when you really need to get approval. One helpful hint comes from the late Bill Gore, founder of Gore Associates, makers of Gore-tex and much more. He developed the "Waterline Criterion," which says: "If it makes sense to drill holes above the waterline of the ship, just do it. But if you want to bore holes below the waterline so we might all sink if you make a mistake, check with the boss first." When considering a bold and possibly provocative action, apply the "Waterline Criterion."

COME TO WORK EACH DAY WILLING TO BE FIRED

When we asked successful intrapreneurs if anything made them different from their peers, over 50 percent answered with some version of "I come to work every day willing to be fired." Whatever could they mean? They don't do foolish things to annoy the hierarchy, and few get fired. They are talking about an attitude that helps them maintain the courage needed to be an innovator.

Fear of authority is hard-wired into the human brain. If we didn't have it, we probably wouldn't survive childhood, because we wouldn't listen to our parents' warnings and the rules needed to keep us alive. As we grow up, we are meant to outgrow this fear, and be disciplined instead by our experience and by higher impulses such as the desire to contribute and get along with the tribe. But schools and corporations and other modern institutions generally keep the fear of authority strong well past the age at which it fades in most hunter-gatherer societies.

The situation is analogous to the domestication of animals. In general, domesticated animals have arrested emotional development. A mature golden retriever, for example, has the personality of a wolf puppy. Both are full of tail wagging and the submissive desire to please. Wolves, however, grow out of this phase. Though a mature wolf may make a good companion, it is not easily kept in a submissive role.

The corporate system tends to produce "domesticated humans," still unreasonably fearful of authority. To become "wild" or independent enough to be a successful innovator, you must manage your fear of authority. The first step is understanding the limits of "Their" power over you.

They can fire you, but they cannot take or even ruin your life. Look upon getting fired as a major inconvenience—one that you would certainly survive, and perhaps even benefit from. The fired intrapreneur has already acquired the skills and attitudes to create another job or his/her own business. The fate to avoid is becoming an out-of-work bureaucrat, since unemployed bureaucrats are in excess supply. For this reason, the bolder approach to work characteristic of the intrapreneur may in fact be the best way to insure that you will always have the skills to support yourself.

Finding your courage is an essential part of full adulthood. Take stock of your talents. If you are fired, your family won't starve. Your kids will still be able to go to college. You will be OK. On the other hand, if you abandon your dreams, you will already have the dead-end job you dread. Act as if your company wanted the best you have to offer. If they take you up from time to time on your intrapreneurial efforts, you will have a worthwhile career. If there is no place for your imagination and energy where you work, you don't want the job anyway. The greatest risk is becoming someone you don't want to be.

BALANCE REALITY AND THE DREAM

The intrapreneurial challenge is to find the middle path: to firmly grasp a worthwhile dream in one hand and reality in the other. Then, with courage and discretion, to use all your accumulated cunning, talent, and knowledge of the system to find a way to turn that dream into a worthwhile reality. This task is never easy, but it's immensely satisfying. To begin, choose a moderate-risk challenge. You can do it!

CHAPTER 4

WHAT AN INTRAPRENEURING
PROGRAM LOOKS LIKE

WHAT CAN A LEADER DO to create a more intrapreneurial organization? This chapter addresses ways to introduce intrapreneuring to an organization that needs to be more
innovative.

A typical intrapreneuring program includes:

1. Sharing the business strategy that calls for and gives direction to
   innovation
2. Creating implementation channels for intrapreneurs with ideas that
   align with the strategy
3. Supporting the launch of intraprises with sponsors, training, and
   coaching
4. Diagnosing and improving your climate for innovation

In this chapter we will discuss the first three. The climate for innovation is the subject of Chapters 12 and 13.

SHARING THE STRATEGY

Intrapreneuring is most effective when it aligns closely with the strategic intent of the organization. For this reason, it is best to begin any
intrapreneuring program by widely disseminating a clear idea of what

you hope the organization and its intrapreneurs will accomplish. Use many different media—speeches, e-mail, breakfasts, posters, in-company magazines, and most of all actions—to make clear what the organization needs to achieve. At the end of each communication of the vision, *ask for help getting there.*

You got to where you are by knowing the answers. As a leader communicating a vision, you need a combination of knowing and not-knowing. You need to communicate both confidence in the overall direction and a completely open mind about how to achieve the ultimate goal. By admitting that you don't have all the answers, you empower the rest of the organization to find them. Otherwise, they would wait to be told what to do.

CREATING CHANNELS FOR VOLUNTEERS

After you tell people you need help figuring out how to achieve the vision, be ready with channels that potential intrapreneurs can use to respond with ideas for implementing the strategy. This is not a suggestion system. Suggestion systems work if the ideas called for are minor improvements that fit well within the existing pattern of the organization.

The kind of divergent thinking a good vision calls forth will overwhelm a suggestion system. Some poor middle manager will be deluged with hundreds of suggestions for new products and other breakthroughs, each of which would take weeks to check out. Instead, build channels that assist would-be intrapreneurs who want to work on implementing their ideas, as opposed to idea people who just want to turn them over to others for execution.

In every organization we have studied, there are plenty of people with good ideas who are trapped beneath layers of hierarchy. If you ask for innovation and don't get much response, you have not created sufficient channels through which new ideas can surface. Good channels are safe for intrapreneurs to use, help unknown intrapreneurs get around the initial resistance of their bosses, and ensure broad distribution. Here are two examples:

SEED MONEY FUNDS

Many companies create a channel for new ideas by setting up seed money funds. A seed money fund is outside the normal chain of command and can give individuals with ideas a small sum (perhaps $500 to $25,000) to begin testing them out. This money is generally used for a quick prototype, travel, or some initial market research. Seed money funds create broad opportunities for participation but leave responsibility with the applicant, thereby testing for commitment and follow-through. Once the seed money is spent, the innovator must return to more normal channels to obtain further funding.

Seed money funds play an important role in liberating the intrapreneurial spirit of the organization. They take away the excuse "My boss doesn't like the idea." One can always get around the boss by applying for a seed grant. A seed money fund thus introduces the idea of multiple options. Strict hierarchy does not prevail if there are institutionalized ways to get around it. We often find seed money funds resisted by line managers—until they see the results.

One line manager was irate as he told us: "Something is wrong here. I told my subordinate that his idea was no good and then you gave him seed money for it. I want you to take it back." Six months later, this same line manager became an enthusiastic champion of both the intrapreneur's idea and the seed money fund when the improved process justified itself and provided both many millions of dollars of annual savings and the basis for a major new product.

We have seen two kinds of management of seed money funds:

1. The seed money fund is managed by a small committee, which takes applications and awards grants.
2. The fund is split into a number of smaller funds, each of which has its own manager. This more decentralized solution is appropriate when the intrapreneurs to be empowered are in many different locations.

There may be significant advantages to each kind, but we have seen great success with both. DuPont and 3M had excellent results with the committee type. Texas Instruments divided up the money and distributed it throughout the organization so that it was easy to access. Again, the results were impressive.

THE INNOVATION FAIR

An innovation fair is a very cost-effective way to sort through a large number of ideas and intrapreneurs. Would-be intrapreneurs display their ideas in small booths. Potential sponsors and teammates, as well as the curious, tour the fair, stopping to chat at the booths that interest them. The event both creates the network needed to move forward and makes a very visible statement about support for innovation. However, if it is to work, it must have good participation by senior management. For example, at 3M, senior executives, including the CEO, spend at least half a day at the annual technology fair.

Innovation fairs come in many varieties. We have helped set up internal innovation fairs with elaborate demonstrations of new technology and booths whose graphics rivaled those seen at a serious trade show. We have managed innovation fairs whose booths were little more than displays of hand-lettered posters with an occasional bench-top demo. Both have their place, but if your goal is to provide a channel for the intrapreneurs whose ideas do not yet have much management support, we suggest that you explore the more modest end of the spectrum.

We often combine an innovation fair with a quick briefing to potential sponsors on their role. Here is a design for a one-day innovtion fair of the most basic sort.

	INTRAPRENEUR TRACK	SPONSOR TRACK	ATTENDEE TRACK
MORNING	Get briefed on intrapreneuring program (1 hour).		
	Design and create their booths (with help).	Receive briefing (1 hour).	
LUNCH			
AFTERNOON	Sell their ideas from booths, Recruit sponsors and teammates.	Tour the show looking for ideas and intrapreneurs they might sponsor.	Tour the show looking for new ideas and things they might get involved with. Build network relationships.
AFTER THE FAIR	Follow up on leads and continue recruiting teammates and sponsors.	Nominate intrapreneurs to an intrapreneur start-up workshop.	Help projects that interest them. Join one of the intrapreneurial teams.

The one day includes not only the fair but also preparation by the intrapreneurs of their "poster show" booths.

The subsequent nomination of selected teams of intrapreneurs to an intraprise start-up workshop sends a signal that something has happened as a result of the fair and gives strong support to the nominees. Among the criteria for proceeding on to the workshop, we generally include at least the following:

1. A member of management has agreed to coach the intrapreneur and provide a bit of "get smart" money to the project.
2. The intrapreneur has recruited at least two team members who at a minimum are willing to pursue the idea for the duration of the workshop.

TRAINING IN INTRAPRISE START-UP WORKSHOPS

One of the best ways to enliven the intrapreneurial spirit in an organization is to use training to launch a number of visible intrapreneurial teams that can be counted on to succeed. Almost all organizations have many potential intrapreneurs with good ideas on how the company could move toward its vision. Given some help, coaching, and support, many of them will succeed.

Most would-be intrapreneurs need a bit of help in subjects such as:

- Recognizing and bringing out their intrapreneurial nature
- Discovering customers' real needs
- Taking the measure of the competition
- Positioning their offering in the competitive marketplace
- Selling, and managing the sales process
- Getting support in a large organization (e.g., recruiting and keeping sponsors)
- Developing a high-performance team
- Creating a business plan

TEAM-BASED ACTION LEARNING

Most intrapreneurs don't relish spending time in an academic setting. Intrapreneurship training works best as team-based action learning. In our best design, two to fifteen teams of three to eight members go through the action learning together, each team working on challenges such as studying customers' needs and creating a financial plan. They learn what they need to know for each task just in time to do it.

Three benefits of team-based action learning are:

1. Participants often go into training as a group of individuals and emerge as a committed team with a common vision.
2. Individuals often come in unsure of themselves as intrapreneurs and emerge having awakened their intrapreneurial passion.
3. The ideas that enter at the beginning are forged in the fire of feedback from faculty, customers, sponsors, and visiting venture capitalists. In the end, the team will have anticipated and avoided many potential obstacles and moved from an idea to a concrete and well-researched business plan.

An intraprise start-up workshop usually consists of three instructor-led segments, with two to four weeks for homework between each live segment (see chart on next page). The homework segments may or may not include on-line coaching. If the teams are truly global and travel is an issue, the live instruction can be offered in two longer segments. The advantage of having three separate live sessions is that the format allows for two major revisions of the business plan. We have discovered that the quality of the business plan is more reflective of the number of revisions than of the time spent on each one.

WHY FOCUS ON BUSINESS PLANS?

In our most successful intraprise start-up workshops, the teams learn intrapreneuring in large part by working together to create a business plan for their enterprise. Intrapreneurial teams know they need a business plan and are motivated to produce one. The plan both pulls together all the diverse issues of creating an enterprise or launching a new product and transforms the workshop from a training into a forum for getting help with the work that needs to be done.

THE VENTURE CAPITALISTS

We generally bring in a venture capitalist or two at the end of an intraprise start-up workshop to critique the business plans and recommend to management which teams to fund. Preparing for a presentation to a venture capitalist raises the adrenaline level and shifts the focus of business planning from what participants believe it takes to get approvals from executives inside the company to what it will

| SESSION 1 | HOMEWORK | SESSION 2 | HOMEWORK | SESSION 3 |
3 DAYS	3 WEEKS	3 DAYS	3 WEEKS	2 DAYS
The nature of the intrapreneur	Research on customers, competitors, etc. to answer questions raised by the first attempt to write a business plan	Surprises, difficulties, and learnings	More learning about customers and competitors	Surprises, difficulties, and learnings
Customers		Teamwork review		Dress rehearsal of final presentations
Competitors		Pricing	Reevaluation of basic premises	
Value propositions		Risk management	Building sponsor relationship	Feedback and modification of the plans
How business plans get written	Team collaboration on-line and in person	Sales management	Teamwork	Presentation to the venture capital panel
Development timeline	Additions to the team	Sponsors	Fine tuning of business plan	
Financial plans	Preparation of revised business plan presentation	Presentation of revised business plans		Planning of next steps
Rapid prototype business plans				Secrets of successful intrapreneurs
Business plan presentations and feedback		Feedback and creation of 2nd interim research plans		
Venture team				
Interim market research plan				

Program for Intraprise Start-up Workshop

really take to succeed with customers in the marketplace once those approvals are won.

USING AN INTRAPRISE START-UP WORKSHOP
TO IMPLEMENT A VISION OR STRATEGY

Our client was a divisional manager in a major multinational. He developed a new strategy and went from site to site explaining the strategy and asking for intrapreneurial volunteers with new product or new venture ideas that would move the division in the direction of the strategy. Anyone with an idea he or she wanted to work on that fit the strategy was invited to an open-enrollment School for Intrapreneurs. As the date of the workshop approached, we were told to expect around twenty-five participants. One hundred seventeen would-be intrapreneurs showed up.

We explained the rigors of intrapreneuring and gave people permission to drop out. A few did, deciding that intrapreneuring was not for them, at least for the moment. We then used a self-selection process to form teams. Some participants dropped their idea to join with another intrapreneur whose idea attracted them. Others combined similar individual ideas into a team idea better than any of the original ones. In the end, fourteen teams completed the training and received funding to launch their intraprises.

This process of strategy implementation was far more rapid than the methods other divisions of the company were using. While the other divisions were still creating and screening project ideas, the intrapreneurial division launched six of the fourteen ventures and developed significant revenues. Using this process, the division set a new standard for rapid implementation of a strategy.

The secret of the intrapreneurial strategy launch is harvesting the ideas and energy of the whole organization to implement the strategy. Using all the knowledge distributed throughout the organization, it was possible to implement the strategy in a way that made good sense down where the rubber meets the road. The other divisions each assigned a small team to study markets and invent products and services from scratch and with few creative resources or ideas but their own. Intrapreneuring is much faster and comes up with much better ideas because the collective technical and market knowledge of the whole organization greatly exceeds that of even the brightest group of strategic planners. And more important still, when you select ideas that already have intrapreneurs, you gain a significant head start, because many months of work have already been devoted to them.

ACCELERATING EXISTING NEW PRODUCT VENTURES

A chemical company used a variant of an intraprise start-up workshop to accelerate existing projects. The projects selected for its School for Intrapreneurs had already consumed a million or more dollars. The training acted as an accelerator of progress.

In the course of five years, the company put over 150 existing new product ventures through the School for Intrapreneurs. A typical project had been in existence for a year or two and at the time of the workshop had a team of five. Three benefits accrued:

1. In the process of converging on a common vision and business plan, team members from different functions discovered that they had had very different notions of where the project was going. Once they agreed on a common vision, work was better integrated and progress was much faster.
2. A number of projects were proceeding on the basis of minimal market understanding. Simple as it seems, helping participants get their attention off technology for long enough to check out potential customers and create a business model produced some major direction changes. Some projects died during the workshop when market research proved basic premises to be false and no new vision could be found to replace the original one. Many more teams changed direction toward more promising markets and different uses for the new technologies.
3. The average team reported an acceleration of three to six months in its progress toward implementation.

Much of what we have done in helping intrapreneurial teams is a long way from rocket science. Simply asking the right basic questions early in the process can make a big difference. Only one warning needs to be given here: use people to teach intrapreneuring workshops who have business acumen and a good track record in the start-up stage of innovation. Both the psychologically astute trainer without business experience and the seasoned manager of mature businesses generally lack the background to ask the right question *about a new venture* at just the right moment.

BUSTING BUREAUCRACY WITH INTRAPRENEURIAL START-UPS

The U.S. Forest Service asked us to help them become radically better at achieving their mission of "Caring for the land and serving people." Their task was made more difficult by a steadily declining budget, increasing demands for their services, and rising standards of environmental responsibility.

To succeed, they had, among other things, to become much more efficient. This meant finding a way to cut through bureaucracy and focus on getting the work done.

As in almost all large organizations, most of the people in the Forest Service do work that is used by other parts of the organization rather than directly by the organization's external customers. For example, a biologist might do a wildlife survey that is used by others to develop an environmental impact statement. That statement, in turn, may be used as part of a planning document that is ultimately used by the Forest Supervisor to manage the forest in ways that serve the public.

In the civil service tradition, the way these tasks were coordinated—or not coordinated—had discouraged rapid innovation and rising efficiency. With declining resources, growing work, and stagnant productivity, important tasks ended up not being done. The environment and the public were not being served as well as everyone had hoped.

As head of reinvention for Region 5 of the U.S. Forest Service (California and the Pacific Islands), Mike Duffy was given the task of finding breakthrough ways to improve performance. Earlier work by a national Forest Service reinvention team and Region 5's administrative reorganization proposal had suggested the use of "enterprise teams" to provide internal services with more intrapreneurial flair. Duffy decided to try this radical approach—to treat the line officers who used internal services as customers and *provide them with choice among alternative internal vendors of those services.*

With the inspiration and support of Forest Supervisor John Phipps and organizational development expert Leigh Beck—among many others—Duffy used an intraprise start-up training workshop called "The Reinvention Accelerator" to launch twenty-one enterprise teams. Each team became a profit center, with internal customers who chose whether to purchase the team's services or not.

Among the services provided by the Forest Service enterprise teams were:

■ Preparation of environmental impact statements, including presentations at public hearings
■ Recreational planning
■ Resolution of worker's compensation cases
■ Archeological assessments and the development of public education programs for appreciation of the archeology of specific sites
■ Timber cruising and scaling
■ Conflict resolution facilitation
■ Library services
■ Fundraising for public/private partnership endeavors
■ Training in a variety of subjects
■ GIS (Geographic Information Systems) mapping and database management
■ Fire management
■ Statistical analysis and modeling

The teams went through a program similar to an intraprise start-up workshop covering the launch of a new product or business with external customers. The major difference was that their customers were mostly inside the Forest Service.

Going from civil servant to intrapreneur is quite a challenge, but we found no lack of intrapreneurial spirit within this government agency. Within a month of completing the workshop, over half the teams were booked up many months in advance. After the reinvention team explained the new system, many line officers used to dealing with bureaucratic staff monopolies welcomed the opportunity to use internal providers who genuinely saw them as customers. They also found that they could reduce costs because they didn't need to employ someone full-time to do a job that could be done, as needed, by an enterprise team. And having plenty of customers, the teams saw no need to stretch out the work.

As Forest Service intrapreneur Jeni Bradley put it: "It has been long enough now that I can tell you how it really feels to be the owner of the *best enterprise business in the Forest Service!* I am having so much fun that I can't even begin to tell you! We are totally booked with work and I am in search of talent to add to the team."

The enterprise team experiment was successful for several reasons:

▩ Strong support by leaders and internal customers who knew what it would take to overcome the immune system of the federal government.
▩ The establishment of an intracapital bank that provided a system for exchange between the teams and their customers and gave the teams the ability to store money earned in good times for use in periods of reduced work or for investment in new services.
▩ Reinvention laboratory status for Region 5 that allowed system designers to apply for waivers of any Forest Service regulations that got in the way of creating a free intraprise system within the agency.
▩ Strong partnership with the union, the National Federation of Federal Employees, which saw internal enterprising as an alternative to outsourcing and played an active role in both designing the rules and selecting the ventures.
▩ A small, highly dedicated reinvention lab staff that coached and championed the enterprise teams as they hit bureaucratic and other more typical start-up obstacles.
▩ A strong desire on the part of participants, their line-officer customers, and the senior leadership to serve the overall mission.

As we write, the experiment is expanding and moving beyond Region 5 to other parts of the Forest Service. Most of the teams are doing very well. If the Forest Service can cut through bureaucracy and bring innovation and intrapreneurship to the everyday tasks of a federal agency, then this basic prescription for innovation is ready for widespread implementation in commercial organizations where the bureaucratic barriers are far less severe.

In large organizations, almost all work is directed to serving others within the organization. How do we get these internal service providers to become more innovative, efficient, customer-focused? The primary answer: give their internal customers a choice among a number of internal intrapreneurial suppliers and let those intraprises sell their services throughout the organization.

In the future, we predict that most employees of large organizations will work in internal service intraprises. However, line organizations will still be in control because they will have the budget. As customers of the internal service intraprises, they will get what they need to achieve their organization's mission.

When in charge of their own internal profit centers, service intrapreneurs will gravitate to where they have the highest value. Through customer feedback, they will learn how to meet their customers' real needs faster, better, and less expensively. The results will be a thoroughly intrapreneurial organization and breakthroughs in innovation and productivity. (See Chapter 14 for further exploration of these trends.)

COACHING THE INTRAPRISES

After a successful intraprise start-up workshop, many of the teams will require additional support with the challenges of implementation. It is advisable to provide some ongoing coaching. Also helpful are reunions at six-month intervals to check in on progress and identify any common barriers that are holding the teams back. Following the progress of the intrapreneuring teams is a powerful way to diagnose your climate for innovation. The unnecessary obstacles that teams keep hitting are indicative of the barriers that are inhibiting innovation more generally. Fix the system.

TRAINING SUBJECT MATTER

Over the years, we have refined our understanding of the subject matter intrapreneurs need most. In this section, we suggest the key components to include if you are designing an intrapreneurial training program.

Am I an intrapreneur?

Buried within nearly every person, or at least within nearly every person likely to show up at an intrapreneuring workshop, is what we call the "inner intrapreneur." However, in most adults the inner intrapreneur has gone into hiding. The parts of oneself that are needed for successful intrapreneuring were probably punished both in school and later on at work. One of the glories of intrapreneurial training is that it is not too difficult to get would-be intrapreneurs to see and make friends with that intrapreneurial part of themselves. When the inner intrapreneur emerges, faces light up and someone will express an insight that is obviously shared by many: "And I always thought there was something wrong with me! Now I know I'm just an intrapreneur!" Once they see this capacity, recognize its value, and practice using it, it's hard to get the genie back in the bottle.

What customers really want

The majority of participants come to an intrapreneuring workshop thinking more about what they will offer their customers than about the benefits those customers will receive. Get participants talking with and understanding potential customers. Get them to watch customers in the situation where the team's product or service will be used.

What is needed is not a degree in marketing but rather comfort in gathering information directly. Encourage workshop participants to talk on the phone, to interview prospective customers about what matters to them, to create day-in-the-life scenarios both with and without the new product or service. We have seen breakthroughs occur when students build a cardboard mock-up of a new product and get potential customers to role-play the selling situation using the cardboard mock-up. It's just enough reality to evoke a deeper response than one could get from any number of words. Use your creativity to help participants experience how their potential customers think and feel.

Defining the offering (value propositions)

To the average early-stage intrapreneur, his or her offering is almost indescribably beautiful. And therein lies a problem: without a succinct *description,* an intrapreneur will get nowhere. We get our students to work on ten-word headlines, elevator speeches, telegrams, and value propositions. The goal is to succinctly state what is most important about their offering in words others can easily understand. In just a few words, what is the offering, who is it for, and who and what is it *not* good for?

Identifying and understanding the competitors

If the average intrapreneurial student is a bit weak on customer understanding, he or she is generally worse on competitors. It is not uncommon for highly technical students to start out by saying, "We have no competitors. There is nothing in the world like what we have invented." The most important thing they must learn is that the customer always has a choice. Simply listing current and potential competitors can trigger a major revelation. Researching them will introduce a strong dose of reality.

Sales and sales planning

In sales and sales planning, the simple stuff often helps. Take your students through the basic stages of the sale, including:

- Establishing awareness of and and positive regard for your offering
- Generating leads
- Qualifying leads
- Understanding what the specific customer really needs
- Explaining the offering
- Handling objections
- Closing
- Post-sale support

How much time will each step take? What are the costs involved? How many leads will they need to get the number of closes they want? Stay in this sales process zone until you begin to get some numbers that will later be useful in the financial plan. If students bog down and claim it is all unknowable, give them permission at this stage to just make it up! Then have them check for consistency. An internally consistent "fantasy" is a step up from a broad-brush concept.

How business plans actually get written

For many beginning intrapreneurs, it is a mystery how business plans get written. They don't have nearly enough information to be able to put down answers to the kind of questions addressed in business plans. Share this dirty secret with them: business planning begins with "making up" the numbers. The early-stage plan is little more than fantasy. You begin with the dream and work backward toward reality. This process sharpens the questions you need to answer. The next step is to check the plan for consistency and plausibility. Have your students fix the inconsistencies and implausibilities they find. Then direct them to begin researching the assumptions that bother them most. Gradually, they replace fantasy with fact.

When they are done, their plan will still contain errors. All innovation plans do. Something will confound their expectations. But the team's understanding of the business and the coherence of the team vision will be far greater if they have imagined in detail and written down what they plan to do. The effort makes them smarter about their options and risks. Then, when the surprises come, they will have a strong enough conceptual framework to be able to respond rapidly. They will know what those surprises mean to their plan and to their chances of success.

DEVELOPMENT PLANNING

Get the team to work on a development timeline. What are the product or service development milestones, and when do they expect to reach them? The timeline, even without fancy analysis, will reveal sequencing and critical-path problems. It will raise the priority of some items and allow the team to postpone others. And it will begin the process of detailed imagination that will make the numbers in the financial plan more realistic.

OPERATIONS PLANNING

Lead the participants through the process of delivering value to a customer. What are all the steps? Ask them to take a wild guess at the cost of each step and figure out the contribution of that step to their unit costs. Next add the sales projections to the timeline. Do the sales goals fit with the development timeline? Then look at the operations implications of those sales numbers. How many people will be required to deliver the volume of sales in each time period? Sales and operations models should be adjusted as needed.

Then spend some time on overheads. Intrapreneurs almost always underestimate them, so give participants lists of possible overhead items and check their numbers for plausibility. What are the direct and indirect costs of operation? Are there ways to become more efficient?

What do the costs need to be if the product or service is to be truly competitive?

Pricing

Have participants establish prices by a variety of methods. What value will the customer see in their offering? (In other words, what will the market bear?) How can they differentiate their offering to increase its value? What do their costs suggest they need to charge? Is there a profitable space between these two? If there is a big potential profit, how soon will that profit attract other suppliers? Is it best to skim the cream or price lower and make life hard for those who will consider developing a competitive offering? Let the class discuss the best pricing strategy for each venture.

Financial planning

Many intrapreneurs believe that creating a financial plan is too hard for them. Our experience suggests that if they can add and subtract, and if they can imagine their business in detail, then with a bit of help they can create a financial plan. The task of the faculty is to convince students that the biggest challenge is imagining the business in detail, not the conversion of that vision into numbers. Once they get over the idea that others have some financial magic that they lack, they can create the spreadsheets that will indicate the financial potential of their business and the critical variables that must be controlled to keep it profitable.

Risk management

Create risk management exercises that give teams good feedback on the risks others see in their enterprises. Then have them develop plans for managing the most disturbing risks.

Managing the corporate immune system

Intrapreneurs often need coaching on how to handle relationships with those who hold some sway over their destiny. There are a few basic lessons to be taught, such as "Ask for advice before asking for resources," but the bulk of the value delivered to students on managing the immune system is specific to the individual and the team. Watch closely as they deal with others. Help them to see how certain habitual relationship styles could be changed in the direction of greater effectiveness. Also, help them to guess who will respond negatively to their ideas. Whose ox is about to be gored? Who loses face if they succeed? Can they find win-win solutions? If not, it's good to know these things in advance and to seek out the allies that will be needed if a confrontation arises.

THE VENTURE TEAM

Have the teams identify the skills needed for the success of their intraprise. Are all the ingredients there? Which individuals and what skills need to be recruited?

Pay close attention to the dynamics of each team. Are the members working together constructively? Is the leadership struggle getting out of hand? If the team isn't working well together, deal with it early on by spelling out team operating principles and calling out any deviation from those principles. Ask the team to fill out and discuss The Team Effectiveness Checklist (Appendix E) several times during the progress of the workshop. Is cooperation improving?

If the chemistry just won't work, find a way to change the membership of the team. If that is not possible, don't fund the team! Let it end with the workshop. Bad blood in teams is the death of ventures. Our most unpleasant failures in intrapreneurial training have come about when we ignored bad team chemistry that was readily apparent during the workshop. Don't do it.

INTRAPRENEURIAL TRAINING IS NOT SO HARD

In general, what is needed is not sophisticated understanding of all the areas involved in conceiving, launching, and running a business. Rather, intrapreneurs need the courage to take on all the diverse subjects in the art of management. To paraphrase Joe Mancuso, "If an intrapreneur does 80 percent of the things needed to succeed 100 percent perfectly, he will surely fail. If he does 100 percent of the things needed to succeed only 80 percent well, he will probably succeed." The trick, then, is to convince your aspiring intrapreneurs to summon the courage to do those necessary things that they don't do well. It is far more comfortable for them to spend their time on the things they do best. However, in that way lies certain failure. As intrapreneurs, they are the self-appointed general managers of a new idea, and as such, responsible to see that everything necessary is done. Since people outside the team will be reluctant to take on big jobs, the team must learn and take care of all aspects of their venture.

To succeed in the training of intrapreneurs, remember these few points:

1. Help them to find the courage they need to succeed.
2. Give them honest feedback about what needs to be improved in their plans in a way that leaves them feeling they have made good progress and confident that they can fix whatever is wrong. Speak of next steps, not past failures.
3. Honor self-selection. Encourage people who don't believe in the venture to quit. Let there be no reluctant intrapreneurs.
4. Watch the immune system and protect your intrapreneurs.
5. Watch closely for the deeper values that drive people in the direction of greater contribution to the company and society. Acknowledge and honor those impulses. Don't assume the motivation is all rational profit-maximizing. Intrapreneuring is too demanding to run on that weak an energy source.
6. Watch the team dynamics and make use of team-building exercises.
7. Express gratitude to the brave souls who volunteer for your intrapreneuring program.
8. Make sure there is strong sponsorship for intrapreneuring. Otherwise quit. Don't lead lambs to the slaughter.

PART TWO

FROM IDEA TO PROFITABLE REALITY

CHAPTER 5

FINDING A GOOD IDEA

INNOVATION BEGINS with an idea. How can you be sure the one you have chosen is right? An idea may be a good business opportunity, yet not be good for you. It may fit you and your company perfectly, yet have a fatal technical flaw. It may be new, exciting, and patentable, yet not succeed in the market. It may fit the market, but not the culture of your organization.

There are so many different ways an idea must be right that you have to consider lots of apparently good ideas to find one worth pursuing. "You have to kiss a lot of frogs to find a prince."

GENERATE LOTS OF IDEAS

Everyone can be creative. The main trick is to stop suppressing your ideas. Once you have done that, give your mind the right stimulation and ideas will flow.

NOTICE WHEN YOU ARE MOST CREATIVE

When do you tend to get your good ideas? In the shower? Driving a car? Riding a horse? Sailing? Fishing? These are all times when the brain is able to run free without feeling it is wasting time. Give your mind permission to roam.

GIVE YOUR SUBCONSCIOUS A CHALLENGE

Present your mind with a difficult problem, be positive about your chances of success, and then give answers time to surface. Be clear enough about the questions and the answers will come.

ENJOY IDEAS FIRST, JUDGE THEM LATER

Learn to love all sorts of ideas. Play with outlandish ideas, silly ideas, and irrelevant ideas. When they first appear, the best ideas often seem crazy, funny, or weird. And in their current form they probably are, because they probably still contain fatal flaws. But sometimes, after playing with a "crazy" idea for a while, you or someone else will see how to fix the flaws. Then its originality and daring become virtues.

ASK GOOD QUESTIONS

Posing a better question is half of the challenge. Can you take a larger view of the problem that allows for more innovative solutions? For example, after noticing that many people are not trying to be very innovative, we might ask, "How can we motivate people to be more innovative?" However, if we expand the framework of inquiry, we notice that the problem is not so much lack of motivation as that the bureaucratic system is blocking or punishing innovation. The solution lies in removing the barriers. So a better question is, "How can we liberate the people in the organization so that they can express the innovative drive that already lies within them?" But that formulation of the question ignores the fact that total freedom leads to chaos. So perhaps an even better question is, "How can we both liberate the intrapreneurial spirit and focus it on a coherent strategy?" This question is more likely to lead to breakthroughs than the one we started with.

BRAINSTORMING

First, define a problem worth addressing. Then, working in a group of five to seven very different people, see how many ideas each of you can write down in five minutes. Don't stop to judge! Shoot for at least twenty ideas each in that time span. Then, as you share ideas, one from each person around the circle, build new ones off the base of those that are offered. Appreciate each other's ideas. Enjoy the game!

Use children, artists, and experts from tangential fields. For example, in solving a problem in mining, we used not only various kinds of mining engineers but also an expert in the biomechanical structure of digging insects. Breakthroughs came from comparing the removal of coal from a narrow seam with the way various insects dig.

Take a silly idea and find ways to make it better

Consider the strengths of an apparently silly idea. How can you make it stronger? Consider its weaknesses. How can you fix them?

Broaden your interests

Innovations generally occur when we combine seemingly unrelated information in new ways. For example, Edison brought together photographic film, the light bulb, optics, and mechanics, each well-known but separate fields, to produce the movie projector. Study a new subject. Take an interest in your kids' music. Talk to people from other parts of the organization about what is going on in their areas. It is easier to be creative if we keep learning on many fronts.

Carry around a note-taking medium

Once you open the floodgates, ideas will flow into your mind, but they will flow out just as fast. When an idea grabs you, write it down. Consider 3 × 5 inch file cards in a shirt pocket, a micro-recorder, a small spiral pad—or a palmtop computer.

Choosing an Idea

Once you get the engine of idea generation running, you will find yourself with a surfeit of ideas. How do you choose which ones to invest your intrapreneurial energy in? If you are working for someone else, there are three areas you must consider.

Does the idea work for the customer?

Early on in the idea evaluation process, talk to customers, not so much to find out whether your idea is good or bad but rather to reshape it, to make it better. Take the position that learning from customers is more important than preventing the loss of secrets. Carry a sheaf of confidentiality agreements if you must, but talk with customers.

Does the idea fit the company?

Ask whether the idea fits the core competencies and strategies of the company. Does it have the scale and rhythm of the things the company does well? Can you imagine someone who might sponsor it? Even with a great idea, don't waste your time if your company will execute it badly.

Does the idea fit with you?

If you are being creative and observant, you will come up with many ideas that are good for both the customer and the company, but if they don't fit with who you are, they are of little use to you personally. Early in the process of screening ideas, ask, "Do I have any skills, experience, or talents that will be useful in carrying this idea forward?" More important, since intrapreneurs never have all the credentials for the tasks they undertake, ask yourself, "Does this idea excite me enough to bring out my hidden talents and my hidden reserves of courage and determination?" If the answer is no, look for greener pastures.

In some cases you may have a great idea that fits the company and the customer, but it is clear that, for whatever reason, you are not the right intrapreneur to push it forward. Your job in such instances is to identify and recruit someone who does have the needed qualities. This is not an easy task. There are far more good ideas than intrapreneurs to carry them out. Finding an adoptive parent for your idea is made easier if you are willing to let the other person look upon it as his or her own offspring.

The interest test

Entrepreneurial guru Robert L. Schwartz of the Tarrytown School for Entrepreneurs used to give each idea that seriously caught his fancy a cigar box. Every time he came across an article or news clip related to the idea or had a new inspiration concerning it, he would drop it in the cigar box. He let this go on until he began to have trouble closing the lid. At that point he figured he had enough enduring interest to begin taking the idea seriously.

In the early stages, your interest in an idea may be a better guide to potential than any test question. If you are deeply interested, keep probing until you find something worthwhile. Do you have a system for tracking which ideas persistently interest you over a period of months or years? Continuing interest is a clue to what is worth following up on.

Chapter 6

Getting Started

When an intrapreneurial idea begins to take hold of you, resist the temptation to tell everyone about it in the grandest terms. Publicity triggers the corporate immune system. Grandiosity excites deep fears.

Practice modest communication

If you tell someone your idea is so revolutionary that it will change everything for the better, they may well believe the first half of the prediction—"that it will change everything"—but they will likely reserve judgment on whether such wholesale change will really be "for the better." Most people presented with an idea of vast significance that could lead to glory or disaster will choose to study and delay rather than either kill it or authorize decisive action. The key to getting quick approvals in the early stages of innovation is to align with the desire to learn more before taking the important decision. In essence, you must communicate: "This decision to proceed isn't dangerous; it is only authorizing a test. The important decisions will come later when we have more information." Then surprise them with success.

Rule 1: Begin explaining your idea modestly. Stifle the instinct to trumpet its virtues. Instead, go to trusted friends and ask for advice about potential concerns, flaws, ways to make the idea stronger, and the next steps to take. Work out some of the conceptual bugs and political issues before exposing the idea to its probable enemies.

Rule 2: Network internally. Intrapreneurs enjoy a sizable advantage over their entrepreneurial cousins: they have many colleagues possessing diverse skills, experience, and outlooks with whom they can candidly discuss their idea without jeopardizing its proprietary status. Gather advice and information from internal sources. Refine your concept. Then go back to the most helpful individuals for more advice, thus laying the foundations of a network of internal supporters.

Rule 3: Explore externally. As soon as internal networking begins to clarify critical issues, it's time to extend your exploring to the world in which your customers and competitors live. Through colleagues, obtain referrals and introductions to customers, distributors, suppliers, and so on. Uncover information sources by talking with outsiders who have broad overviews and large networks, such as specialty magazine editors and trade association officials.

Many first-time intrapreneurs are apprehensive about initiating outside contacts, but when they do, they are usually surprised and relieved to discover how easy it is. Most people are happy to talk about their areas of expertise. The hardest part is making the first call. The main rules to follow when contacting strangers for information and opinions are:

- Never try to sell the idea—look for ways to improve it.
- Accept all suggestions graciously.
- Ask for the names of two other people who might help.

Expect that some of the feedback from knowledgeable outsiders will be negative. When this happens, try to find solace in the fact that you are learning and discovering potential problems early, when they are easy to fix. As you find solutions to these problems, your enthusiasm will rebound. Expect this sort of emotional roller-coaster. It is an unavoidable part of intrapreneuring.

Build financial models early

Intrapreneurs are frequently surprised to hear us say that the time to start building a financial model of the new business is in the early concept-development stage. They object that there isn't enough hard data to support a meaningful profit and loss projection. They are right, but there is much to be learned by trying. By playing with the numbers, you learn about what you have to accomplish to turn your project into a successful business. This is worth knowing early on.

The intrapreneurial way of setting up an early-stage P&L spreadsheet is to:

1. Make up numbers as best you can. (Tip: search out and adapt "rules of thumb" used in similar businesses, often found as ratios, e.g., sales expense/revenue.)
2. Check for interdependencies and correct inconsistencies.
3. Note what assumptions you make when guessing at numbers.
4. Investigate those assumptions, especially the ones that make you nervous when you write them down.
5. Based on what you learn, make better-informed guesses. Substitute these new numbers in the spreadsheet.
6. Check the picture for consistency and fix the internal contradictions.
7. Continue checking assumptions.
8. Gradually replace guesses with better-qualified estimates.

Actually, this process continues all the way through business start-up and beyond:

9. Take action.
10. Measure what happens.
11. Revise estimates to reflect actual results.
12. As the world surprises you, keep making revisions in your financial model.

The initial financial model guides concept development by highlighting the most critical assumptions. It helps identify the best timing for key milestones and where speed-ups are necessary.

The first financial projections for a new venture are like the first layout sketch for a new mechanical design. The sketch lacks detail, but it shows the most critical pieces and how they will work together. The financial model shows how development costs, variable costs, fixed costs, and capital costs work with pricing, sales projections, and timing, thus providing an indication of the venture's financial returns.

We have seen too many venture teams put off financial analysis until their product is nearly developed. They don't discover serious problems with their business model until it is very difficult to change course.

Finance is the language of business. Learn to speak it.

IDEA SCREENING

We have found it extremely useful in our work with venture teams to have them evaluate their business proposition and development progress by considering three basic questions. We're sure that we did not originate this technique, but we have used it so many times and adapted so many versions of it that we have lost track of where we picked it up. Now, on behalf of all innovators, we extend a "thank you" to whoever first formulated these three questions to evaluate a new business proposition. The questions are:

- Is it real?
- Can we win?
- Is winning worth it?

Begin gathering evidence to answer these questions as soon as a new business idea begins to take shape. As the business develops, keep asking them.

IS IT REAL?

Recognize real business opportunities by these signs:

- You have identified real customers—not in a vague way that includes half the population but in terms specific enough to single out individual prospects.
- You have identified and checked out the distinct benefit to be delivered. Your targeted customers want it.
- Your offering is clearly better in some important way that customers will value.
- A technically sound way exists to deliver the benefit with room to make a profit, at a price customers appear willing to pay.

A business proposition with these characteristics is likely to be real—that is, a viable business for someone. The next question is, Is it a viable business for you and your company?

CAN WE WIN?

Winning the game of new business development means beating the competition. Being just as good, or marginally better, won't do. To displace existing competitors, you must be noticeably better.

For over twenty-five years we have been counseling clients to introduce new products with an "unfair advantage" by exploiting capabilities that competitors can't match. We began using the term in this context at a time that coincided with the early auto racing exploits of entrepreneur extraordinaire Roger Penske.

Penske's racing organization was then enjoying phenomenal success. Its competitors loudly ascribed that success to possession of some "unfair advantage," and the media followed along.

Others were developing racing technology within the boundaries of generally available and gradually evolving knowledge. Penske's organization was feverishly exploring new territory with the help of some outside research labs. They achieved breakthroughs in unraveling the complexities of vehicle dynamics, which they exploited in subtle but significant refinements on their race cars.

The result was that Penske's cars did have an advantage, but it was not an unfair one. No rules had been violated. The advantage was "unfair" only in the sense that competitors couldn't match it.

In business, perhaps the most straightforward example of an "unfair advantage" is possession of a meaningful patent. Usually, however, such advantages are achieved in more subtle ways through some unique business capability or combination of capabilities.

But to gain a true "unfair advantage," uniqueness may not be enough. Winning in new business development also depends on achieving a competitive superiority that can be sustained. Imagine a new product idea that passes all the tests for realness and is based on some highly proprietary technology. It may look like a winner, but it won't win if a competitor responds by rapidly implementing a different technology that works even better.

How long do you think your offering's superiority will last? Is there a competitor that might be better equipped to succeed once the new product or service becomes known?

To win in the long run, you need an "unfair advantage" that will enable you to start and stay well ahead of others. The competitive environment will not remain static. Your new offering will stimulate competitive responses and may even encourage new competitors to enter the market. Consider all of these factors in evaluating your prospects of winning.

Is winning worth it?

Let's assume that you have developed a new business proposition that is real and exploits the weaknesses of potential competitors. For good reasons, you believe you can win. Before pushing the Full-Speed-Ahead button, however, there is one more basic issue to consider: will winning be worth the struggle and cost?

The obvious way to address this question is to estimate the development and start-up costs, the timing, magnitude, and profitability of future sales, and from these the projected financial returns (for example, net present value, internal rate of return, return on capital employed, economic value added). To be sure, these financial parameters are an important part of the answer, but they are not the complete answer. It is also important to consider the risks and weigh the hoped for returns against gains that might be realized through other uses of the resources your venture would consume. Investing in your project means that your company will not be investing in others.

Besides beating the external competition, you must compete with other internal projects that are vying for the same resources. Weighing all the pluses and minuses of competing venture propositions may not be something you can do alone. Nevertheless, recognize the issues involved and be sensitive to the perspective and concerns of your "investors."

Most executives wrestling with new venture funding decisions go beyond financial analysis to consider issues such as:

- How well does the new business support the company's long-range strategy?
- Might the new business stimulate the growth of other related businesses?
- Are there any unusual risks associated with this business?
- How does the new venture compare with other ventures already under development—where does it fit in the "venture portfolio"?

The way to address these issues is not to sit back in your ivory tower. Make guesses (hypotheses), then get out in the world and test them. Explore and learn. If you remain convinced that winning will be worth it, figure out how to help others to see what you see.

CHAPTER 7

AVOIDING TYPICAL
NEW PRODUCT MISTAKES

Make your mistakes faster.
                    —*Don Gamache*

THE SECRET OF cost-effective product development is really not to avoid mistakes. It is to make mistakes sooner and learn faster. Mistakes made early can be easily and inexpensively corrected. If you hold tenaciously to your preconceptions, the cost of changing later can be huge.

The key to cost-effectiveness is to *accelerate the learning process* by testing the critical assumptions as early as possible. Useful early-stage "assumption testers" include:

- Discussions with prospective end users
- Construction and evaluation of a demonstration model
- Small-scale market tests with "prototype" samples
- Joint development with a potential customer
- Hands-on evaluation of competitive offerings
- Simulations

With innovation, surprises are inevitable. Things never turn out quite as we expect. *The job of an intrapreneur is to uncover the major surprises as rapidly and cheaply as possible.*

Major changes in the later stages of development not only waste time and money, they may also waste a sizable chunk of your career on nonproductive work. Big surprises discovered downstream in the development process may even result in project-stopping disasters.

SOME COMMON MISTAKES

Since innovation never proceeds according to plan, managing it in a bureaucratic way usually fails. People in bureaucratic workplaces tend to perpetuate mistakes rather than change their plans. They associate changing plans with admitting they were wrong, thereby exposing themselves to reprimand—or worse. Instead of reinventing the idea with each unpleasant surprise, they continue on their mistaken path until a glaringly obvious failure shuts them down.

In supportive climates, successful intrapreneurs are willing to expose themselves to the risk of early-stage mistakes. They then overcome them by learning, adapting, and forging on. In the early stages of new product development, there is no other technique that will produce more or faster learning than this "try it, fix it" approach. The fear of taking action and learning from mistakes is the characteristic that most dramatically distinguishes the less innovative from the intrapreneur. Risk-averse climates stifle innovation.

The result of not forgiving and adapting to "honest mistakes" can be very expensive failures. *Not tolerating and learning from early-stage mistakes is about the biggest mistake you can make.*

Although mistakes made and discovered early are often helpful accelerators of progress, the same cannot be said of mistakes discovered late in the development process. These mistakes can kill a project. Usually these deadly downstream surprises result more from mistakes of omission than from mistakes of commission—more from things that were overlooked than from things that were done in error.

We have also noticed that when such surprises strike, they tend to spring from one of four deficiencies. These are what we call "The Four Deadly New Product Mistakes":

1. Market misunderstanding
2. Lack of an intrapreneur
3. Strategic misalignment
4. Slow execution

MARKET MISUNDERSTANDING

A common omission, often fatal late in the development process, is the failure to sufficiently differentiate your new product from competing products in your customer's eyes. To you, of course, the distinction may be incontrovertible. We are no longer surprised and only mildly amused when we ask an inventor about the competition and they say, "Well, what's really great about my idea is that no one has ever done anything like this before. It has no competition." To experienced investors and sponsors, this statement tells little about the merit of the idea but volumes about the naiveté of the inventor.

In reality, customers always have a choice. Perhaps there is no direct competition for your new high-speed amphibious car, but many people get some of the same satisfactions from the combination of a car, boat, and trailer. They can and do spend their money elsewhere.

Business is the art of delivering benefits to customers. Without reference to a customer, all any product or service can offer, no matter how clever or technically advanced it may be, is features. Only when a feature contributes directly to the well-being of a customer does it becomes a benefit. As one of our students in a School for Intrapreneurs once observed, "It's a feature if we've got it—it's a benefit if they want it."

Too often, inventors become captivated by clever features they create and stop short of developing products that offer superior benefits. It is a bitter lesson when prospective customers reject their clever invention because they see the new product as no better than one they already know and trust.

We offer this advice to all inventors: know your customers and design with them in mind. Maximize the perceived customer benefits and *eliminate extraneous features that add cost.* Make sure your offering provides a benefit worth far more in your customer's eyes than you will have to charge to get a good return on your company's investment.

LACK OF AN INTRAPRENEUR

The danger when management endorses an idea and sets up an implementation team is that the appointed leader may not be an intrapreneur. Without the monomaniacal focus, courage, creativity, and willingness to face feedback of an intrapreneur at the helm, a great idea may well run aground.

AN INTRAPRENEUR SUCCEEDS WHERE A LINE MANAGER FAILED

Early in our work with intrapreneuring, we were hired to help a cement company deal with a growing "mountain" of waste cement dust. The EPA had started fining the company for not handling it. For years they had tried "selling" the dust—essentially, giving it away for the cost of moving it. There were several known uses for the material, but they could find no consistent customers. They had concluded that the identified applications weren't viable.

They asked us to uncover new uses for the dust. We identified quite a few, but our screening revealed that the previously known ones (for example, a base for agricultural fertilizer) had greater potential than the company was assuming. When we dug deeper into how these applications had been pursued, we learned that a well-respected line manager had been assigned the job of selling the dust, which he undertook in addition to his other responsibilities.

We suspected that previous efforts to sell the dust had failed because the company's traditional bureaucratic approach lacked intrapreneurial leadership. We advertised inside the company for a venture leader. We interviewed many candidates and picked a fire-breathing intrapreneur.

He did his homework and developed an innovative business plan to attack some of the known applications with a clever franchised distribution strategy. At our suggestion, the company had us put together an incentive plan for his venture that balanced the tangible risks of failure with an "appropriate" reward for success. The incentive structure we suggested was based on the intrapreneur's business plan.

Our client, with the intrapreneur's best interest at heart, became concerned that the reward formula was based on selling the entire daily production of two hundred tons of waste dust—a herculean task. "We would be very pleased if he sold 10 percent of that," they said. We therefore sweetened the reward system using twenty tons a day as the target. Soon the intrapreneuring program was in trouble. Guess why.

Within six months, the new intrapreneur was selling four hundred tons a day. After his venture consumed the daily production of waste dust, he started mining the mountain of old dust. When he ran low on usable material from this source, he began hauling away dust from rival cement companies.

His business was moving twenty times the projected volume that formed the basis for his incentive plan. The incentive formula kicked out a bonus that made the intrapreneur the second highest paid employee in the company, ahead of all the vice presidents. The immune system closed ranks—crying something about an "unearned windfall"—and six months later the intrapreneur was gone.

This experience taught us three lessons that have been confirmed many times since:

1. Bureaucratic approaches to innovation don't work.
2. Never underestimate the power of an intrapreneur to get spectacular results. (But be sure you have a good one.)
3. Financial risk and reward should both be more modest for intrapreneurs than for entrepreneurs. (Eyebrows rise when your intrapreneurs appear on the 10K among the top ten highest paid officers.)

WHERE TO FIND INTRAPRENEURS

Some executives believe that intrapreneuring will not work for them because there aren't any intrapreneurs in their organization. We have enjoyed watching such skeptics become believers. Belief blossoms as they approve funding for a business plan created by volunteer intrapreneurs who were helped along by some encouragement and training.

Here are some suggestions for bringing latent intrapreneurs to the surface. Even in the most bureaucratic organization, there are more of them than you may imagine.

■ Describe your strategies and visions in an inspiring way.
■ Advertise internally for intrapreneurs who have ideas that will help to implement those strategies.
■ Take the best of the volunteers, help them form small teams, and give them a training program that teaches what it means to be an

intrapreneur and coaches them through the creation of a well-supported business plan.

- Encourage managers to become sponsors of the intrapreneurs.
- Screen the business plans and invest in the best, assigning the team that wrote the plan to its full-time execution.
- Maintain this process and it is unlikely that you will ever run out of intrapreneurs.

INTRAPRENEURS: MADE OR BORN?

We are frequently asked, "Are intrapreneurs made or born?" They are mostly made, though innate predisposition may play some role. We have often seen people who had exhibited no apparent sign of intrapreneurial personality become successful intrapreneurs when their passion was aroused and the circumstances left no other route to success.

We asked one such intrapreneur what had inspired her dedication. She told us, "I was tired of having my ideas shot down. I knew this was a good new product for the company. I decided I was not going to let this idea lie down and die. I promised myself that I would turn it into a successful business or get kicked out of here for trying."

NURTURE INTRAPRENEURIAL TEAMS

Many new product and business development failures are the result of not having a real intrapreneur in charge. Many other failures come from not forming, trusting, and supporting intrapreneurial teams. To avoid these kinds of failures:

- Don't back a "team" that is a team in name only.
- Coach the team in the intrapreneurial role and watch to see that it continues to function cohesively.
- Spend enough time with the team to develop confidence and trust in its thinking. Help by asking open-ended questions, but allow the team to reach its own decisions (unless it appears to be heading for catastrophe).
- Knock down barriers that get in the team's way. Use the team as a diagnostic to find and fix areas of bureaucratic viscosity that are slowing progress for everyone.

If you are a part of a new product team, ask yourself, "Is this team led by an effective intrapreneurial leader whose judgment and commitment I trust? Am I grabbed by this idea in a way that brings out my own intrapreneurial spirit?" If the answer to either question is no, start looking for another assignment or another job. Never accept an intrapreneurial role if your heart isn't in it.

If you need to innovate, you need intrapreneurs. Create the right environment and intrapreneurs will come forward. Don't try to innovate without a passionate intrapreneur dedicated to the project. Take the time to find them and have the courage to empower those intrapreneurs and teams you decide to sponsor.

STRATEGIC MISALIGNMENT

The key question for an intrapreneur to explore relative to his or her *external customers* is: Will the customers recognize enough value in the benefit(s) this product offers to buy it at a profitable price, even though there are other acceptable products they could buy instead?

Similarly, the key *strategic alignment* question an intrapreneur must answer is: Is there an internal customer who recognizes sufficient strategic value in this innovation to devote resources to its further development and launch, even though there are known alternative uses for these resources?

While a few "between the chairs" ideas will succeed with corporate support alone, connection to the strategic intents of existing business units is the most reliable foundation for strategic fit. Are you able to explain why one of your company's business units should invest in your project?

Successful intrapreneurs identify the decision makers who will ultimately determine the fate of their innovations. They test their assumptions with these leaders early in the development process. This avoids the most common strategic fit mistake: going forward with development without some assurance that the new product will have a home.

CHECKING YOUR IDEA FOR STRATEGIC ALIGNMENT

Some companies have clearly defined strategic intents, missions, visions, plans of action, and core competencies. Others have missions or visions written down, but in terms so general and vague that they provide little direction, or, even if clear, have little to do with how decisions are made.

If decisions in your company are guided by well-defined strategies with some longevity, you need to learn all you can about them.

- Ask for the references (books, articles, documents) that define the strategy terms as they are used in your company.
- Learn to understand the written strategies and what they mean in practice.
- Develop and gravitate toward ideas that align with enduring corporate and business unit strategies.
- Find out who the champions of those strategies are and ask them for advice.

EXPLOITING CORE COMPETENCIES

Over the past decade we have seen many corporate strategies that call for the leveraging of "core competencies." A core competency is a difficult-to-duplicate collection of capabilities that work together to create an enduring competitive advantage across a spectrum of businesses. Ideas can often gain support by aligning with these competencies, particularly ideas that fit between or cross boundaries in the organization.

A classic example of a core competency is Honda's proficiency in designing, manufacturing, and marketing products powered by small engines. Honda exploits its small-engine core competency in many different businesses, including motor cycles, cars, lawnmowers, outboard motors, and home generators.

Many of the design, manufacturing, and marketing lessons learned in any one of these businesses can be applied in most of the others. Thus Honda has a competitive advantage over companies operating in just one or two of these business domains.

For other companies, core competencies might stem from combining skills and capabilities in areas such as:

- Design
- Distribution systems
- Manufacturing facilities, capacity, and/or location
- Proprietary technologies
- Marketing
- Manufacturing process secrets
- Sales

- Supplier partnerships
- Raw material sources
- Customer relationships
- Company and brand image
- Technical service

If your organization is consciously developing core competencies, and if your idea exploits or extends one or more of them, you may be able to gain support from those who have interests in developing those competencies further.

WHO WANTS TO OWN YOUR VENTURE?

Exploiting core competencies is important, but not sufficient, to assure that a venture meets the test for strategic alignment. The key is to determine who wants the business when it grows up.

In one of our intrapreneuring workshops, we watched a very dedicated team present a computerized training business that was far from the focus and style of the company's other businesses. The venture was already running and was attracting some significant outside customers. The "sponsor" was present, so we asked him if he would continue to support the business in a year if it met all its targets and needed money to grow.

"No," he replied, "it doesn't really fit this company's culture."

"But then why support it now?" we asked.

"I don't want to disappoint these people," he replied.

After reflecting on how much more disappointed they would be after investing another year of their lives in the project, we took the team aside and suggested that another area of intrapreneuring might be more productive unless they could develop stronger support for their divergent strategy. The team redirected its focus and became very successful in another area of software development that had obvious long-term strategic fit with the company's orientation.

If executives in a line business are enthusiastic sponsors, you can be confident that your venture offers a good fit with the unit's current business style, culture, plans, and aspirations. If these executives are willing to fund its development out of their own budgets, you are well on your way. If your venture also leverages strategically identified core competencies or takes the organization toward a stable strategic intent, it has a good chance of continuing to pass the strategic alignment test in the future.

SLOW EXECUTION

In new business development, the most common execution mistake is to move forward so slowly that windows of opportunity close before the product or service can be launched. The world presents a constantly evolving set of opportunities. Open opportunities today become the well-defended turf of established competitors tomorrow. To succeed in this environment, intrapreneurs must aim ahead of the target of opportunity and launch before it moves out of range.

Trusting an intrapreneurial team is the most effective weapon an organization can employ to reduce response time. Our studies of innovation case histories in many different industries reveal an alarming fact: two-thirds of the elapsed time in new business development projects is frequently wasted while the project team waits for approvals and resources.

True intrapreneurs, being cut from the same cloth as successful entrepreneurs, work around such absurdity. They use their courage and creative abilities to find ways to move forward and maintain progress. Yes, they bend a few rules, but only in matters where mistakes are affordable, and never for unearned personal gain.

Intrapreneurs naturally want to focus their efforts on the external environment—their customers and competitors. They network effectively across boundaries to obtain help and support. If one person or group won't help them, they find someone else who will. All told, an empowered intrapreneurial team can get things done in less than half the usual time.

In companies that manage innovation well, sponsors speed projects along by creating a protective bubble around intrapreneurial teams to let them focus on getting the job done. Teams need strong sponsors to protect them during the dark days when their project is taking the most flak.

If you can be such a sponsor, do it. If you are more senior, make sure that being an effective sponsor of innovation is highly valued. Make it a key factor in promotion decisions.

The saving grace of successful intrapreneurs is *sound business judgment.* They know where to draw the line. They apply Bill Gore's "Waterline Criterion," introduced in Chapter 3. As you will recall, Gore gave his people permission to bore holes in the company "ship" and asked only that the boss be informed before drilling below the waterline.

Gore said the only problem he ever had operating this way was that some innovators underestimated the corporation's freeboard. He felt they sometimes didn't use all of the discretionary latitude he was trying to give them.

Trustworthy intrapreneurs know where the waterline is. They will not put major resources at risk without official approvals, and they never compromise safety or environmental standards. True intrapreneurs are also brutally forthright and honest. For obvious reasons, career bureaucrats often see them as subversive mavericks.

STAY AHEAD OF THE CURVE

Winning at new products and services is not for the faint of heart. In many of the fastest-moving industries, one must commit to action long before the hard data needed to justify expenditures is in.

A classic example occurs in electronics. As soon as a novel product hits the market, competitors begin building the next generation. If the pioneer company that created the new product waits until its financials prove the new thrust is sound, competitors will start the next generation first and soon steal the market. At Hewlett-Packard, they say, "First generation products never make money. If you aren't willing to start developing the second generation well before the first generation appears in the market, don't bother with the first generation."

USE KEY MILESTONE PLANNING

We use a key milestone timeline to help project teams respond faster. To start, the team imagines the major milestones on the path to successful commercialization. We make sure that all relevant aspects of the business development process are considered (technical prove-out, patent strategy, customer testing, market research, business/financial planning, process design, scale-up, and so on). Then the team arranges the milestones in a workable sequence on a timeline.

For "hardware," we use Post-it® notes and a paper-covered wall. The paper is ruled-off in vertical columns denoting appropriate planning increments. For near-term steps a column might represent a week. As the planning horizon recedes, a column might represent a month, quarter, or year. See the figure on the following page.

Each Post-it® note describes one milestone. It is easy to make changes and move milestones around. Colors can be used to indicate classes of activities and/or priorities.

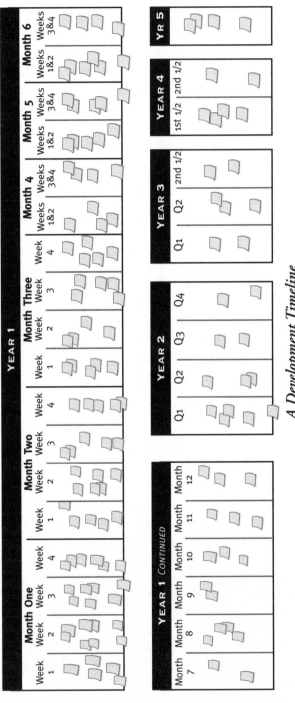

A Development Timeline

This system's primary virtues are that it is large enough and simple enough for a whole team to see and work on at once. It encourages the team to explore "what if" ideas and highlights any holes in the implementation plan. Each team member is exposed to the whole-system view of the entire development process. Some teams leave their timeline hanging in a "war room" where it is always available for reference and updating.

We encourage teams to set realistic yet challenging time goals. Applying the 80/20 rule—80 percent of new information is usually generated by the first 20 percent of the work—we prompt teams to streamline tasks and tackle new ones well before preceding steps are complete. As the schedule takes shape, we challenge the value of each step to ensure that work is focused on the most critical milestones. Some steps are combined, run in parallel, or eliminated.

ACCEPT SOME RISK FOR THE SAKE OF SPEED

After their first pass through this process, teams generally feel that they have created an aggressively streamlined development schedule containing a just-tolerable level of risk. At that point, we ask them to find a way to get to critical milestones *at least 30 percent faster.*

We acknowledge that moving faster will probably remove safeguards and suggest that they specifically look for ways to take on more risk in exchange for speed. The result is frequently paradoxical: *A little more risk often buys a lot of time, and cutting time to market reduces risk!*

A MATERIAL SPEED-UP

We worked with a team that had invented a revolutionary new material. It had produced a small amount of this material using a multi-step "batch" process and bench-top apparatus. The resulting sample quantities were adequate to verify the material's unique properties but insufficient for trials with prospective customers.

An early look at process economics showed that the experimental batch process would be too expensive in production to meet the cost objectives for commercialization. Instead, a continuous manufacturing process would be required. The team believed that developing a continuous process would be challenging but feasible. To test this assumption, it had obtained funding to develop a small continuous-process demonstration line. The plan was to subsequently ask for more funding so that the line could be expanded and sufficient material made for customer trials.

From an engineer's perspective, this two-step approach seemed prudent. But having adopted a more intrapreneurial perspective during our "accept risk to save time" exercise, the team changed its plans. A decision was made to postpone proving the feasibility of a continuous process. Instead, the authorized funds were used to scale up the batch process. And rather quickly, enough material was made for meaningful customer trials.

The team changed its plans because it had more doubts about its ability to predict customer response to the new material than about its ability to manufacture the product if the demand was there. It proved the most critical assumption first and thus was able to get substantial funding to develop a continuous process and scale up faster in the end.

As long as the risks of potentially catastrophic consequences are well managed, doing some things "wrong" is often a faster and cheaper way to learn. When you figure out how to get smarter faster, you usually discover a lower-risk and more cost-effective approach to your innovation.

We shudder when we hear innovators proudly say, "We are taking the time to do things right." Time is too valuable to spend on such ego-gratifying frivolity!

CHAPTER 8

INTRAPRENEURING WITHIN A STRUCTURED DEVELOPMENT PROCESS

FOR AT LEAST a century, companies have been developing processes to institutionalize virtually every function in business. The movement is rooted in the work of Frederick W. Taylor at the turn of the century. Known as the father of scientific management, Taylor believed that there was one best way to perform every job. In recent years, this belief is moving into the area of innovation processes. However, process standardization works better in routine activities than in the management of innovation.

Like Taylor, some still maintain that *all* work is a process. But is courage a process? How about integrity, perseverance, creativity, respect, and trust? If these are not processes, then the right process is not the whole answer for effective and efficient innovation, which cannot be achieved without them.

Although some have tried, no one has yet developed a process that assures commercial success in new business development. We believe that no one ever will. Innovation, like the creativity that fuels it, requires spontaneity and the freedom to go in new directions when interesting discoveries beckon.

Having said that, we wish to strongly support work on innovation processes. Studying innovation processes can lead to innovation climate improvements that eliminate a lot of unnecessary barriers and delays. But it is critical to develop your process so that it supports the way innovation *really* happens.

Three key aspects of supportive innovation processes must be borne in mind:

1. The process must serve the people who drive innovation, not vice versa. The drivers of innovation are the intrapreneurs, cross-functional teams, and active sponsors who make it happen. Leave room for them to configure the process to fit the idea they are developing.
2. In innovation, there are always surprises and setbacks. The process must recognize the value of early-stage mistakes for the lessons they teach and not seize on them as reasons to cancel projects or disrespect intrapreneurs.
3. The most supportive innovation processes contain several process models. Innovators choose the one that most closely fits their circumstances and then modify it as needed.

Today, most intrapreneurs are obliged to follow some sort of institutionalized innovation process. There are good ones that facilitate commercially successful innovation. Unfortunately, there are also bad ones that stifle innovation with needless bureaucratic protocol. We have seen both.

WHY HAVE A STRUCTURED INNOVATION PROCESS?

The effective management of innovation requires that business leaders work with long-range strategists to guide their company's new business development projects. A process can help management choose a mix of projects likely to achieve long-range objectives. It can help ensure that resources are appropriately allocated among those projects.

Innovation processes generally provide for periodic executive reviews of venture progress. Preparation for these reviews—if not excessively structured—can help intrapreneurs maintain a whole-business perspective. Reviews can raise appropriate questions that even an experienced intrapreneur might miss. A process can help intrapreneurs address the "Is winning worth it?" issue.

An effective process recognizes that good ideas and intrapreneurial talent exist throughout the organization, and pulls them in from all corners. It ensures that innovation does not become the exclusive preserve of some particular group.

A good process guarantees that absolute pass/fail authority is not granted to any single group or committee. It recognizes and encourages every manager as a potential sponsor of innovation. It empowers managers to be effective sponsors of unpopular ideas. It creates and sanctions many breeding grounds for new ideas. It expects line managers to fund many innovations from their own budgets and provides reward and measurement systems that encourage them to do so.

THE "NATURAL" STRUCTURE OF INNOVATION PROCESSES

Periodically, management must review and adjust priorities in its overall portfolio of new business initiatives. If we call such reviews *checkpoints,* and the intervals between checkpoints *stages,* a "natural" stage-checkpoint-stage sequence results. (The discovery of this natural "process" might surprise those who have believed that the more familiar "stage-gate" processes are an invention of management science. Actually, it is almost impossible *not* to have an innovation process of this sort.)

We prefer to call the reviews "checkpoints" because that more accurately describes what they should be: examinations to confirm or tune up a venture's strategy and ensure that it is appropriately resourced. "Gate" implies more of a binary go/no-go barrier that a venture must somehow wiggle through to survive. Unfortunately, that is what gates have become in some of the stage-gate processes we have seen.

WHAT WORKS AND WHAT DOESN'T

- A process that gives power to volunteer sponsors selected by the project teams will probably work.
- A process focused on optimizing the allocation of resources to a portfolio of projects has a good chance of working.
- A process that concentrates on attempting to preclude venture failures will surely fail.

When the focus is on preventing failure, the temptation is to over-engineer, micromanage, and dehumanize the process.

In one extreme example of micromanagement, the process was documented in two volumes, each two-and-a-half inches thick, of procedural details and instructions. That process had many discrete stages, with specific functions to be accomplished at each stage according to a standardized methodology. Different elements of new business development were addressed in sequence rather than in parallel. When all of the basic stages were completed, the various elements were assembled into a preliminary business plan.

The well-intentioned group that administered this process was known by successful innovators inside the company as the "Department of Innovation Prevention." Doing business planning by their one-step-at-a-time process *blocked whole-system thinking.* It tripled the time it took to put a plan together. It also produced plans that took triple the time to execute.

The key to structuring supportive innovation processes is not the isolation and rigorous detailing of the various elements of new business development. Rather, it is achieving integration of these elements in a way that helps managers and teams visualize the business opportunity as a whole system and focus on those risk and opportunity factors most critical to that specific business.

The task of creating an integrated vision of "what matters most" resists being turned into a process. It is accomplished only by using systems thinking and sound business judgment—key attributes of successful intrapreneurs. Thus, supportive innovation processes and savvy intrapreneurs are highly complementary—so much so that it is extremely difficult for one to succeed without the other.

Absent the infusion of systems thinking and sound intrapreneurial business judgment, innovation processes resemble paint-by-numbers exercises. The result may look OK, it might even display real craftsmanship, but it will lack the creative interpretation and "life force" that sets it apart and gives it real value.

The intrapreneurial way of developing a new business proposition is more like sculpting in clay. The sculptor begins by rapidly building up a basic shape on a supporting armature. Then, in an increasingly painstaking way, she adds detail in stages through addition and subtraction of material. More often than not, as details are added, it becomes apparent that major sections must be removed, repositioned, or reshaped to achieve the desired proportions. Gradually, the final shape and texture emerge. The mechanics of the process are easy to teach. Technique can be refined through coaching by experienced masters. In the end, however, only experimentation and practice can develop the intuitive sense of shape and proportion required to achieve praise-worthy results.

So it is with new business development. It is not a linear, deductive process. Success requires savvy intrapreneurs supported by effective sponsors. These sponsors must have time to coach within an innovation process that recognizes the value of intuitive insight and readily accommodates experiments and course corrections.

BEYOND THE "HOME RUN SYNDROME"

Most big businesses start out as small businesses. This is an aspect of new business development that is overlooked in many innovation processes. Particularly in larger companies, innovation processes tend to focus all of the exploratory and planning work exclusively on major, long-range opportunities.

The high potential in these opportunities may provide the justification for proceeding with development, but exclusive focus on the huge can seriously compromise the smaller, near-term "stepping stone" opportunities that are needed to "get smart." Quick small-market exploitations start you on the learning curve sooner, and thereby end up providing an "unfair advantage."

HERCULES AND CARBON FIBER

In the past, when the technology was new, many companies were working in the field of carbon fiber composites. It was universally assumed that the major opportunity for this expensive, high-performance material was in aerospace applications. We were working with Hercules, which shared this belief. Our assignment, however, was to help uncover some short-term specialty applications to launch the product and accelerate the development of applications expertise.

Hercules understood that it would take many years to qualify the new material for production in critical aerospace applications. Its strategy was to gain a head start on its competition.

Their first commercial carbon fiber products were golf club shafts, fly rods, and tennis racket frames. The use of carbon fiber in these products gave end-users some small but demonstrable performance advantage. Some consumers were willing to pay high premiums for this slight edge. These also were products where material failure would not be a catastrophe. By working with manufacturing partners on their development, Hercules uncovered and solved application engineering and component fabrication problems long before the competition.

Hercules was able to charge customers a premium for the material because the initial products were highly valued for their prestige and performance by the "early adopters"—end-users sometimes called the "lunatic fringe." This revenue helped offset development costs. It also elevated the venture's credibility within the corporation.

In the ensuing years, many early Hercules competitors lost patience waiting for the aerospace market for carbon fiber to develop. Unable to compete effectively with Hercules' head start in the specialty applications, they elected to exit the business.

In the mid-1990s, Hercules sold its composites business as part of a corporate restructuring to focus on core chemical businesses. But for over two decades it was among the world's leaders in carbon fiber.

We have seen few innovation processes that encourage a rapid-entry, "get smart quick," staged-introduction strategy like the one that was so successfully employed by Hercules. *An early launch strategy should be considered in every new business development plan.* It should be baked-in to every structured innovation process.

THE ROLE OF CHECKPOINTS

Checkpoints should not be strictly win/lose, pass/fail events. They should be viewed by all involved as opportunities for refinements and course corrections.

We were interviewing a later-stage venture team that had taken its new business into commercial operation about a year earlier. Team members told a story of great initial success followed by a 90 percent drop in sales. "Why did sales drop?" we asked. They said they didn't know.

Only after about thirty minutes of probing discussion did they mention that several months previously they had lost their dedicated sales force. Now they were working through an integrated sales force that was also responsible for many of their company's traditional products—polymers sold by the tank car. The team's products were ultra-high-performance injection-molded parts. It was no surprise that a sales force that thought in tons had little interest in selling high-priced finished parts.

Why didn't the team immediately grasp the probable connection between the loss of its sales force and the decline in sales? The answer, we discovered, was that the innovation process was structured around stressful go/no-go reviews. Let us explain:

The decision to consolidate sales forces had been made at a very high level. The team was told it was not "politically correct" to complain. It was now focused on gaining approval to continue its venture at the next "go/no-go" gate. Confronting the true source of the problems would have angered those whose approval was needed, *so the team literally put the facts out of mind.*

A good innovation process would have helped the team members confront what experience was trying to teach them. It would have focused management attention on fixing the sales problem (perhaps by allocating necessary sales resources) or, if that was not appropriate, terminating the venture "with honor." But the review process was focused on go/no-go rather than exploring what had been learned and what changes in strategy those learnings implied. The result was an indefinite continuation of a strategy that guaranteed an expensive failure. The team's best option: tell the truth and ask either to be given a dedicated sales force or to be allowed to close the venture and find work elsewhere in the company.

Unless a very different tone is set, intrapreneurs whose survival depends on approvals will see gates as *competitions that must be won.* "Getting through the gate" must not become the sole definition of winning. If it is, clever employees will figure out how to win regardless of their project's potential, and resources will be wasted.

Instead, winning should mean the demonstration of outstanding business judgment, development work, and experience-based learning, even if the ultimate conclusion is that the project should be terminated. One of the most impressive checkpoint presentations we have ever seen ended with the team making just such a recommendation. All present applauded the team for the thoroughness of its work and its courage. There was no doubt that this team had won.

PART THREE

THE TRICKS
OF THE TRADE

CHAPTER 9

ADVICE FOR
HANDS-ON INNOVATORS

OVER THE YEARS we have asked successful intrapreneurs about the secrets of their success. Here is some of what we have learned.

BE A COURAGEOUS BUT MODERATE RISK TAKER

Bulletin: Successful entrepreneurs are not high risk takers! They choose what they perceive to be *moderately difficult challenges.* Once committed, they pursue the idea with great courage. They also do everything possible to reduce their risk, such as locking up a distribution channel, forming a key partnership, or supporting the start-up with a related service that generates revenue while they learn. You can be too cautious or you can be too wild. Ask yourself: "If it were my money, would I risk it?"

Capital gives entrepreneurs the wherewithal to take risks. For intrapreneurs, the equivalent of capital is reputation. Your past successes build up the capital of your reputation. How much freedom will your reputation buy? Huge dreams may have to wait until you have demonstrated your ability with more modest innovations.

But don't be too conservative. Consider the time you have left on Earth. You want to do something significant. You want to build your reputation as an innovator, not as a drone. Be bold, but weigh the risks before plunging in. Once in, play hard, but with an eye to survival.

BE FRUGAL, STAY FLEXIBLE

The best intrapreneurial team is the one that learns the most at the lowest cost. Run lots of small experiments. Don't buy fancy equipment if you can kludge up an experiment on existing equipment. Get started and begin learning. Buying expensive equipment too soon locks you into one way of doing things. Keep your options open.

BE CREATIVE ABOUT THE PATHWAY

Bureaucracy believes there is only one right way to move forward, only one place to go for each kind of help or resource. If that were true, as soon as you ran into a nonbeliever with a monopoly on some form of approval or resource, you would be blocked. Fortunately, in the informal organization, there are many places to go for resources, assistance, and feedback. Look for support in other functions outside your chain of command. Develop your options. Be crafty without being dishonest or self-serving. If you believe in your idea, find a way to make it happen.

BUILD A TEAM OF ENTHUSIASTIC VOLUNTEERS

Unlike invention, innovation is almost never a solo effort. Recruit a team of enthusiastic volunteers. Accept appointees if they fit, but fight against accepting people who can't get excited about the idea. However they arrive, make sure everyone understands the vision and strategic intent of the team and has a heartfelt commitment to them.

One way to build commitment is sharing the task of creating a vision. Credit others whenever possible; leaders must suppress pride of authorship. But accept the leader's responsibility to make the tough decisions when, amidst the chaos of new ideas, participation does not bring about consensus. Make sure everyone comes to a clear agreement on subgoals, targets, and each team member's responsibilities. (See Appendix E: The Team Effectiveness Checklist.)

BUILD A NETWORK OF SPONSORS

Every innovation needs a network of higher-level supporters who create a coalition to keep the project alive. Show potential sponsors a "can-do" creativity and the ability to follow through. Seek out managers whose advice you truly value. (See Appendix D: The Sponsor Evaluation Checklist.)

ASK FOR ADVICE BEFORE ASKING FOR RESOURCES

Recruiting people to your cause is best done gradually. If you approach a would-be sponsor and say, "I've got this great idea and I need a big chunk of your budget and headcount," you will be met with resistance. If you say, "I need your advice, do you have five minutes?" most people will say yes. Don't ask if the idea is good or bad; ask for advice on how to move it forward, which in the early stage often means how to check it out.

If someone gives you five minutes of advice, she has already spent five minutes of her time on your idea. Either the idea has potential, in which case that was a good use of the company's resources, or it is worthless, in which case she has wasted her time. Since it is probably too soon to tell objectively whether your idea has real merit or not, anyone who has given you these five minutes is likely to make herself right by believing your idea is worth investigating.

On the other hand, if you ask someone for resources and he says, "No" or "Let's wait a bit," the reverse psychology applies. He has made a good decision only if your idea is mediocre or worse. He will unconsciously devalue the idea to make himself right. Continue to ask for things that are relatively easy to give. Resist making a request that is likely to be denied.

"Ask for advice before resources" applies equally to recruiting team members, requesting temporary help from another organization, putting in for a budget from your boss, or anything else. First establish the pattern of small contributions, then gradually ask for larger commitments.

ACCEPT HELP WHEN OFFERED

THE
GENEROUS CFO

We were watching teams from an in-company intrapreneuring workshop give a presentation to the CEO and CFO of our client. The CFO, normally a rather forbidding man, became excited by one of the teams' ideas, jumped up, and enthusiastically offered to fund the project. The team, which had worked long and hard to cleverly fund the project from inside their division, said, "It's not necessary, we can fund it through the next two stages ourselves." Crestfallen, the CFO sat down. But a bit later in the presentation, he once again leaped up and offered to fund the project. Again the team refused his money.

Since this was part of a course, we called for a time-out. We took the team members aside and said in a stage whisper, "Accept help! If you continue refusing his help, you will eventually make an enemy. If you accept, you reinforce his desire to help you in the future. Which do you want?" They returned to the meeting, accepted the CFO's help, and developed a high-level sponsor. They survived the next round of cost-cutting that might otherwise have killed a very good idea.

In general, you build friends by accepting help. You make enemies by refusing help. Yet there is some "help" you cannot accept. Handle this issue with tact and care.

EXPRESS GRATITUDE

If someone gives you advice, come back later and tell him how helpful it was. This increases the value of his gift and therefore the value of your idea. Even if someone is hostile, find the valuable part of her criticism and later thank her for her help. Gratitude is the universal solvent of opposition. If you keep insisting their actions are helping you, there is a good chance your opponents will come to see themselves as part of your support system.

UNDERPROMISE, OVERDELIVER

Build an aggressive plan with the team and drive yourselves to achieve it. But officially commit to more conservative projections. The bureaucracy doesn't understand that in innovation nothing happens according to plan, so in your official projections give yourself room for a few surprises. The more aggressive plan remains a "secret" that is shared only with team members and an intimate sponsor. With luck, by shooting for the secret plan but revealing only the less optimistic official plan, you will underpromise and overdeliver.

LEARN FROM EVERYTHING

Your job as an intrapreneur is to discover a pattern that works. This will involve lots of false starts and hard lessons. Make those lessons pay. Debrief every failure and every success. Gather your team and do thoughtful postmortems. Ask, "What is there to learn here?" Don't get depressed. Have faith in your ability to learn.

Listen critically to all feedback. Don't "roll over" just because an important person criticizes your idea. What are the facts behind her opinions? Why does she feel as she does? Is she seeing something you don't? Once you understand where she is coming from, you can either change your plan or change the way you present it.

EMBRACE THE BARRIERS WITHOUT LOSING OPTIMISM

Successful intrapreneurs are not Pollyannas. They don't proceed with blind faith. They search both for what might go right and what might go wrong. Embrace potential barriers as interesting problems to be solved. Figure out ways around them. The trick here is to consider potential disasters without losing heart.

DEVELOP BUSINESS JUDGMENT

At the core of the intrapreneurial role is business judgment. There are hundreds of decisions to be made for which good analytical data does not exist, or would be too expensive or time-consuming to gather. So you have to plunge in, make your best guess, and be ready to try something else if you are unsuccessful. Making good decisions usually requires "street smarts" that are achieved only through experience.

How can you learn business judgment when you are not yet in charge? Ask questions. Make your own guesses. Predict outcomes. Track results. Ask yourself, " Why did it turn out the way it did?" Being curious, getting involved, caring about outcomes, taking the time to learn from events—these things are within your power. They will lead you to better and better business judgment .

WORK FOR THE GOOD OF THE WHOLE

As an intrapreneur, you often ask for special favors and special support. Be sure you give back to the organizational community. You can give back by being a leader in the fight for less bureaucracy and greater freedom for innovators. If your intraprise gets a special relaxation of the rules and then goes on to success, you are part of the movement to change the way the company goes about innovation. If you align with the strategic intent, your success is a win for all. If you serve customers' needs in new ways, you are expanding the organization in a way that creates jobs. Even if your innovation is a cost saving, you are liberating resources for better uses.

If you are genuine in your desire to make the whole organization work better, your co-workers will be more likely to see you as a community member rather than as a competitor. Rather than dispute your right to enter their turf, they are more likely to chip in and figure out how they can contribute.

Chapter 10

What You Can Do
as a Middle Manager

To a large degree, the culture of an organization is created by the actions of middle managers. Even large innovations need middle-management sponsors to get them through the early stages of development—only when initiatives have achieved a certain level of concreteness do they merit top management attention. Among smaller innovations, the bulk come to fruition with their primary sponsors still drawn from middle management's ranks. In short, if middle managers don't actively support innovation, very little of it will occur. What can you do?

CO-CREATE A VISION THAT INSPIRES YOUR PEOPLE

The overall vision of the organization is often too general to inspire the innovation you need from your people. Create a more specific vision for your area that demands both continuous and breakthrough innovation. Your vision should stretch your parts of the organization beyond what could be achieved without significant amounts of innovation.

10× TARGETS

Set your unit's sights on a tenfold improvement in specific areas of measurable performance. Motorola has been amazed by what it has achieved by setting 10× targets. When the targets are set, most seem impossible. Yet on average, the company achieves, or nearly achieves, about 75 percent of its 10× goals.

DEPTH SOUNDINGS

Use a participative process to find out what really matters in your area. Ask your people:

- How do we contribute to the overall success of the company?
- Who are our customers?
- What are their needs?
- How might we serve them a whole lot better?
- What could we stop doing?
- What other needs could we fill?
- What new technologies could we use?
- What new skills do we need?
- What other services and products could we provide?
- What should our attitudes and relationship be?

CO-CREATE VISIONS THAT INSPIRE PEOPLE IN OTHER PARTS OF THE ORGANIZATION

In this emerging age of knowledge work and information automation, the role of middle managers is changing. Your job is much less about control and relaying messages up and down the chain of command, and more about tying things together laterally across the boundaries of the organization.

The fact that the job is increasingly one of horizontal integration means that you are almost always working on issues beyond your authority to control. You can't get much done by issuing orders. You have to build coalitions and influence others to get things done. Your job is not only to stimulate the innovation productivity of your own people but also to inspire creativity and flexibility in many other parts of the organization. Build organizational coherence by working across boundaries to create shared visions. Help sponsor intrapreneurs in other areas when their dreams support a shared cross-organizational vision.

ASK FOR HELP IN FURTHERING YOUR VISION

Once you have a shared vision, ask for help in defining it further and making it real. This requires the humility to say, "I see roughly where we must go, but I need your creativity to figure out in more detail what the vision means." Watch to see who volunteers energy, ideas, and action. Express gratitude for all contributions, even if they cannot be used.

BECOME A SPONSOR

As we enter the innovation age, sponsoring innovation becomes central to the role of middle managers. Top management doesn't have the time to guide, to coach, or even to protect one-tenth of the innovation needed. If the organization is to have more than a few innovations, most will have to be sponsored by middle managers and first-line supervisors.

BET ON PEOPLE, NOT JUST IDEAS

Remember what the venture capitalists say: "I'd rather have a class A entrepreneur with a class B idea than a class A idea with a class B entrepreneur."

Look closely at the people who are bringing an idea forward. You may be sure the intrapreneurial team's initial plan won't work exactly. But if the team members are resourceful and committed, they can continually adapt the plan until they succeed.

Here are some good questions to ask before making a major investment: Do these people have the intrapreneurial spirit? Will they work together as a high-performance team? Do they have the essential skills and experience for the job? Do I trust this team to snatch victory from the jaws of defeat?

Learn to recognize and value the entrepreneurial spirit. Here are some hints on telling the difference between intrapreneurs and "promoters"—the venture capitalist term for entrepreneur wannabes who talk a good game but execute poorly.

REAL INTRAPRENEURS	PROMOTERS
Driven by a vision of a better way and the need to make it happen. Use money to keep score on progress toward the vision.	*Driven by a desire for power and position.* See intrapreneuring as a way to get a larger budget, better title, improved visibility and pay.
Moderate risk takers. Once having chosen a challenging and worthwhile objective, study the risks and look for ways to manage and reduce them.	*High risk takers.* Obsessed with the pot of gold at the end of the rainbow. Deflect attention from risks and potential obstacles and refocus conversation on how great it will be when the project succeeds.
Persistent. Once commited to an idea, stays with it even when it's not popular.	*Flash in the pan.* Changes ideas when the going gets rough.
Analytic and intuitive. Use analysis when data is available, but not afraid to use intuition when a decision must be made with less than adequate data.	*Analytic or intuitive.* Predominant use of one or the other of these two thinking styles.
Honest. May be quiet in some situations but always tell the truth and promptly share news, good and bad, with team and sponsor.	*Often dishonest.* Tend to say whatever is necessary to sell the project.

Differences Between Real Intrapreneurs and Promoters

(See Appendix C: The Intrapreneurial Evaluation Checklist. Also see *Intrapreneuring,*[2] Chapter 2.)

KEEP THE CORE INTRAPRENEURIAL TEAM TOGETHER

The system will seek to break up the core team and move members to other projects. While peripheral team members can move in and out as the demands for their talents change, a solid core team contains the memory of lessons learned on the way to discovering a workable pattern of success. The company has paid for an expensive education about one specific idea. Don't throw it away by moving effective members of the core team to other projects.

LEARN TO LOWER YOUR STATUS WHEN WITH THE TEAMS

When visiting an intrapreneurial team you are sponsoring, the greatest danger may be that they will take your offhand comments as commands. You may just be trying to make conversation when you say, "I wonder how it would look in blue." But when you come back next time, the product is blue despite all the market research the team has done showing white is best. You can get close enough to know what is going on—without taking over—only if you lower your status so that you are treated more like a peer than a power-figure. Otherwise, the team loses control, stops thinking for itself, and ceases to take responsibility for decisions. Without knowing it, you become the intrapreneur. If you meant to be only the sponsor, you don't have time to do the intrapreneurial leader's job. So if you inadvertently take over, no one will be truly leading the project and it will soon fail.

One way to lower your status is to, literally, lower your head. Sit down. If you are really powerful, sit on the floor. Speak in a softer voice. Express uncertainty. Show respect for the team's opinions. These actions send semiconscious signals that you are not in charge. Both you and the team members will then naturally shift toward peer relationships. At that point, you can stretch their minds with tough questions and still expect them to do what they think is right.

SPEND CASUAL TIME WITH THE TEAM

Sponsoring is a time-consuming job. You need to roll up your sleeves and spend time with the team in its location. Have coffee with team members. Take an interest in their recent progress, not for purposes of review, but just because the project excites you. By doing this, you learn what you will need to know later when others attack the project and you have to explain what is going on.

Another good ploy is to ask the team to help you prepare for a meeting during which the project may come up. You role-play a tough questioner, and they play you giving the answers. The whole group will get a good laugh and learn the vulnerabilities of the project and how to defend them. You get to introduce tough questions without becoming the "bad guy." Everyone is on the same team.

ASK CHALLENGING QUESTIONS

Challenging, open-ended questions provide a good way to learn about the team without taking over or issuing orders. If you ask, "Why don't you do such and such about unit costs?" this may be heard as a command. If you say, "I'm concerned that we may run into problems on unit costs. What can we do to be more sure of our margins?" you leave room for a wide variety of possible answers. You have raised your concern but left the team members in charge. And you will learn more about how they actually think. Focus on asking good questions and let the team give the answers. Listen as if they know what they are talking about!

BUILD A NETWORK OF ADDITIONAL SPONSORS

As a middle manager, you probably will not succeed as a solo sponsor. Let others think this is their project, too. Help the intrapreneurs connect to others who can back the project and solve boundary problems.

KEEP FAITH WITH YOUR INTRAPRENEURS

If you believe in them, don't let them down. If you are losing confidence in the idea, tell them first. If they succeed, make sure that they are rewarded well. Bolster their careers if they fail in a good and honest attempt. Sponsoring requires mutual trust. Be deserving of their trust.

CHAPTER 11

WHAT YOU CAN DO
IN SENIOR LEADERSHIP

WE ARE ASSUMING that you want to create a fast-moving, innovative organization that takes the world by storm. You want a steady stream of new products and services. You want process innovation. You want old products and services marketed and sold in new ways and in new places. You want continuous improvements and you want breakthroughs. You want to get better and stronger faster than your competitors so that you become and remain the undisputed leader in your industry.

Your company can achieve these things, but not as a bureaucratic organization. To get an explosion of appropriate innovation, you must find a way to release and direct a wave of entrepreneurial spirit. Here are some simple steps that will open wide the doors of innovation.

INCREASE DISCOMFORT WITH THE STATUS QUO

At the heart of innovation is a healthy dissatisfaction with things as they are. Otherwise why change? People in highly bureaucratic organizations become complacent about the company's overall performance. They focus most of their energy on fighting for internal position and a share of the spoils rather than on enlarging the whole. Innovative organizations are dissatisfied with the status quo. People within them focus on challenges such as achieving the mission or serving customers better.

Dissatisfaction with financial performance alone is not the best driver of innovation. It tends to focus managers on devices to increase short-term profitability, and this frequently means killing off innovation projects.

If you really want to raise your own level of dissatisfaction in useful ways, approach the issue more qualitatively. Don't let the system filter out unpleasant truth. Build direct lines to customers, suppliers, and employees. Find a way to carry on anonymous, in-depth e-mail conversations with random employees. Then use the information you glean to fix the larger system, not to hunt down the poor employees' supervisors or department heads.

Adopt a customer and spend time with people in that company. Find out what suppliers think. Get together a panel of the lower-level consultants working within your organization—just you and them, off-site and off the record. What have they learned about how the company functions?

Use the Innovation Climate Questionnaire in Chapter 12 to increase your dissatisfaction with the way your organization goes about innovation. It can stimulate dialogue on ways to improve innovation that build on the organization's cultural strengths and address its cultural weaknesses. You can also use the questionnaire to conduct an annual culture check in all the various areas of the company. You will soon learn which of your leaders are true supporters of innovation.

Once you, as a senior executive, have become truly dissatisfied with things as they are and are determined to make them better, it's time to raise the level of dissatisfaction in the rest of the organization.

CREATE A STRETCH VISION OR STRATEGIC INTENT

It is impossible to give employees the freedom they need to be innovative unless they are guided into alignment by some force other than hierarchical commands. Vision is a powerful tool for aligning the independent, innovative employee.

Create a vision that stretches the organization beyond business-as-usual. A strategic intent that exceeds what seems possible with existing resources inherently calls for innovation. Such a vision or intent demands organizational transformation, not just incremental improvements. It creates new freedoms and new responsibilities because it requires the creative energy of all employees.

A vision must go beyond mere financial goals. Employees will not leap out of bed in the morning to give stockholders a 17 percent return on their investment. They need an inspiring picture of what the company is to become.

ASK FOR HELP

We often attend the annual meeting of the top one hundred officers of a company, and while waiting to give a speech ourselves, we listen to the CEO or the chief strategic planner lay out the strategy for the coming year. Though they give brilliant presentations, too often we see a blankness or weariness in the audience. Why are they not moved?

If leaders are too perfect, nothing happens. As long as the CEO is preaching from a position that says, "I know it all and I hope you all get it," the creativity of the audience is not evoked. Instead, the listeners wait for the all-knowing boss to tell them how the vision affects them and their area of work.

Effective leaders admit that they don't know it all. Though they are sure the directions they point in contain fruitful opportunities for innovation and change, they also know that they need the creativity and intrapreneurship of many ordinary employees to find and implement the specific opportunities that lie within the overall strategy.

FIND OUT WHAT IS BLOCKING INNOVATION AND REMOVE IT

Nothing creates cynicism faster than a senior management team that calls for innovation and then leaves in place the systems and people who are very obviously blocking it. Some suggestions:

- Ask the innovators in your organization who the most damaging knee-jerk blockers of innovation are. Don't promote those blockers. Watch them and, if appropriate, put them on probation.
- Give everyone in the organization "Save a Tree" rubber stamps. Have them stamp and return any form or report they don't need to see. One of our clients saved thirty thousand trees per year with this program. Imagine the savings in hours of wasted work! Imagine the impact on the human spirit of lifting the burden of that huge waste.

- Put together a team to discover obnoxious approvals and forms. Ask who requires them. Mostly, those people are retired or no longer care. Eliminate hundreds of approvals and forms. Post discontinued forms on the cafeteria walls. People have fun doing this, and it gives hope.
- Require every report generated internally to include an estimate of the number of hours that went into preparing it. Often minor requests for information stop real work in its tracks as middle management scrambles to get the most precise answer possible. When the answer to an offhand question turns out to have cost two hundred hours, leaders ask questions more carefully.
- Do an innovation climate audit and handle whatever comes up.
- Put a turf-defending, bureaucratic naysayer's head on a pike. Or perhaps just let the innovation blockers resign quietly. Cruelty may simply raise the level of fear. But don't keep hatchet-men to do your dirty work.
- Create an environment in which people at all levels can get on with the work of turning the vision into a reality.
- Promote only those who sponsor rather than block innovation.

SEARCH FOR AND REWARD SPONSORS

Sponsors are the critical link between top management and the innovators in the organization. They select, fund, nurture, guide, educate, question, and redirect innovators. No system for promoting innovation can replace the courageous and vital sponsor who understands and cares about the idea and its intrapreneurial team. But effective sponsors are generally rare and underappreciated.

Ask yourself, Whose people are innovating? Ask successful innovators, "In your darkest hour with this innovation, who came to your defense? Whose coaching was most helpful? Who used their clout to keep your project alive?" You will discover that a tiny proportion of the company's managers are doing the lion's share of the successful sponsoring. The rest get in the way and/or lack the business judgment to know who or what to sponsor.

Good sponsors have the judgment to recognize an idea before it is obvious. They have the people skills to bring out the best in a team without taking over. They have the selflessness to defend good ideas even when those ideas are unpopular. They are your best candidates for the future leadership of the company.

VALUE BOTH CONTINUOUS IMPROVEMENT
AND BREAKTHROUGH INNOVATION

A company, after a long cost-cutting binge, decided that it could not achieve profitability and growth through cost cutting alone. Therefore, senior management suddenly began calling for new ventures, new products, and new services. Would-be innovators throughout the company responded. Projects began. A few years later, just as the flow of new revenue-generating innovation began to encounter the costs of market introduction and scale-up, senior management decided new revenue initiatives were not producing the results they had hoped for. Someone pointed out that a 2 percent cost reduction in one of the company's major products would do more for the bottom line than most new products. The word went out and divisions around the world began cutting back on new products and putting resources into cost reduction programs. Almost all the new product work was lost as projects nearing success had their funding withdrawn.

To make matters worse, a similar dynamic then occurred in process innovation. It takes a few years to cultivate breakthrough process innovations, so for a substantial period of time only mediocre process improvement ideas were ready for scale-up. By the time breakthrough ideas were nearing implementation, the focus had shifted back to new products and new ventures, and the breakthrough process projects were killed.

In this company, we uncovered a history of three complete cycles from new-product focus to process-improvement focus and back, with each swing killing off most of the existing breakthrough innovation projects. Top management had not intended such abrupt swings, but in each shift of emphasis the message from the top was exaggerated as it worked its way down the ranks. For example, what began as "Put a little more attention on process innovation" became, by the time it reached the shop floor, "Shut off new products and get going at once on reducing costs." The steady oscillation of focus virtually eliminated all process and product breakthroughs.

Keep your system open to all kinds of innovation. Value continuous improvement, process breakthroughs, line extensions, new products and services, new ways of working together, new internal services, and new organizational patterns. While the emphasis may change, all kinds of innovation have their place. Don't plow under the innovation crop before it's ready for harvesting.

CREATE A MUTABLE ARCHITECTURE

The essence of an innovative organization is flexibility. The flexibility needed is not achieved by constantly changing the formal organizational structure. The innovative organization is a constantly changing network of relationships across the formal boundaries. Given an intrapreneurial architecture, people seeking the connections that will enable them to do their best work will adapt the organization on the fly.

Ask yourself, What policies and institutions will foster the most effective self-organizing system? What force fields can I put in place that will guide its evolution toward constructive activities and forms?

BUILD CHOICE INTO THE SYSTEM

To create flexible systems that adapt to the challenges at hand, build choice into the lives of employees. In a bureaucracy, employees wait to be told what to do. In an intelligent organization, employees don't wait; they exercise their freedom of choice.

The following are some examples of choice that you can build into your system:

- Institute a 15 percent rule. In many companies, by policy, employees may spend 15 percent of their work time on new ideas of their own choosing. This lets them test hunches and explore surprises. It improves the quality of employee suggestions because employees have time to check ideas out before bringing them to management's attention.
- Give employees more choice over which projects they work on. Some projects that don't make sense at the practical level will die for lack of staff. Also, you'll find out who the real leaders are—everyone will want to be on their teams.
- Let operating divisions choose how much staff service they want to buy from whom. Not only will costs drop, but staff services will improve. Formerly bureaucratic staffs will get creative in finding ways to satisfy the needs of their internal customers.

The U.S. Forest Service had two technical service centers, each serving half of the country. There were numerous complaints that these regional centers were not sufficiently customer oriented, so the agency gave the various forests a choice between the two. Almost overnight, both centers became more concerned with providing cost-effective services that were valued by their users.

Competition and duplication have a bad name in companies, but in truth, they can be good *or* bad. Political competition for a monopoly right to deliver services or provide components often brings out the worst in people. But when customers have choice, the competition to earn a place in the evolving network brings out innovation, cost consciousness, and a search for effectiveness. (See *The Intelligent Organization*,[3] 186–189.)

BUILD COMMUNITY: BE INTOLERANT OF SELFISH POLITICS

Freedom is the product of a people's capacity to go to the core of their souls and to evoke constantly new and ennobling patterns of meaning and significance.
—*William van Dusen Wishard*[4]

You will find it easier to build choice into the system if you can trust your people to use it for the good of the organization rather than to promote their narrow personal interests. Build community spirit by creating visions of the future of the organization that address people's deepest values. Make the organization stand for something the employees can be proud of—something that makes it worthwhile to rise above selfish concerns and cheer for the whole.

At the core of community is voluntary contribution to the whole, above and beyond the call of duty. Too strict an accounting of time, too brutal an MBO (management by objectives) system, too much focus on narrow measures of performance, and the sense of voluntary contribution suffers. As a leader, you can:

- Respond with gratitude to all volunteer efforts to serve customers and make the organization more effective.
- Create space for individuals to volunteer for team projects outside their normal jobs.
- Make sure all managers understand that the volunteer sector inside the organization is the root of corporate community.

A less pleasant task in community building is discouraging managers who are more interested in fighting over turf than building the strength of the whole organization. But how do you find them?

Looking down from the higher reaches of the organization, you may find it difficult to see which of your people are generous to each other. By contrast, it is very easy for the people below to see which managers are builders of the organization and which are only builders of their own careers. Too often, those who fight for what they believe is right are labeled as "not team players," while those who earn points with the boss at the expense of the organization and its customers are seen as "willing to sacrifice for the good of the whole." Do not be fooled. Know what the troops think of their leaders.

To create an organization that has the integrating force of community, go out of your way to discourage and refuse to promote those who are primarily working to increase their own power. Some hints:

- Be intolerant of finger pointing. Speak strongly to those who blame individuals rather than seeking the root cause of a problem.
- Favor those individuals who correct the systemic sources of problems.
- Build processes to reveal subordinates' opinions of leaders and managers.
- Review the long-term effects of a manager's tenure. If a manager's area falls apart soon after she leaves, she probably created short-term results at the expense of the long-term health of the organization. If many innovative successes were started during her tenure, you had someone who was working for the long-term good of the system.

One division was known as the most "turfy" (turf conscious) in the company. Meetings of the division's functional leaders deteriorated rapidly into finger pointing. Other divisions got little or no cooperation. Rates of innovation and business growth were both unacceptable. The division was being sued for safety violations. Top management replaced the division leader with someone well known for bringing about cooperation and cross-boundary generosity.

The new leader refused to respond to finger pointing by his staff. He always said, "I am not interested in whose fault it is. Let's talk about how we are going to fix it." He noticed and recognized willingness to share and cooperate. Within two years, the division was known as the most cooperative and generous in the organization. Safety problems were solved. Major product innovations had growth back on track.

The central task of a leader is to lift people out of selfishness and local turf defense into a concern for the success of the larger enterprise, the larger community. If the people are attacking one another, the leader has failed.

MEASURE THE RATE OF INNOVATION

You get what you measure and pay attention to. If you want innovation, measure it. It's not easy to do well, but the effort to measure innovation counterbalances the tendency of normal accounting measures to focus people's attention on the short run.

3M measures the innovation output of every division with a "Technical Audit." A team of auditors comes to the division and reviews all the innovations, classifying them on a scale that runs from minor improvements to new "technology genes"—breakthroughs from which numerous superior new products are expected to evolve. The results of this audit, like the financial results, are considered a key measure of a leader's performance.

MEASURE THE CLIMATE FOR INNOVATION

How well are you doing in creating an environment for innovation? Which divisions are doing the best? Which are making progress? Do a yearly innovation environment audit to find out. (See Chapter 12.)

PART FOUR

THE CLIMATE
FOR INNOVATION

CHAPTER 12

DIAGNOSING YOUR CLIMATE FOR INNOVATION

G REAT LEADERS CREATE conditions that bring out people's ability to produce extraordinary results. Central to that task is creating a climate for innovation, which is a force field that guides managers and intrapreneurs toward innovation—or toward giving up on it.

This chapter examines nineteen Innovation Success Factors that together create the conditions for cost-effective innovation. The following chapter presents methods of strengthening each of these factors.

THE INNOVATION SUCCESS FACTORS

1. Transmission of vision and strategic intent
2. Tolerance of risk, mistakes, and failure
3. Support for intrapreneurs
4. Managers who sponsor innovation
5. Empowered cross-functional teams
6. Decision making by the doers
7. Discretionary time
8. Attention on the future
9. Self-selection
10. No hand-offs
11. Boundary crossing

12. Strong organizational community
13. Focus on customers
14. Choice of internal suppliers
15. Measurement of innovation
16. Transparency and truth
17. Good treatment of people
18. Social, environmental, and ethical responsibility
19. Avoiding the "home run" philosophy

We have audited these factors in many organizations and found them to be fundamental measures of organizational health as well as capacity for innovation. The questionnaire we have used to measure these nineteen innovation climate factors is at the end of this chapter. Use it both as an introduction to the concept of climate for innovation or as a tool for checking out that climate in your organization.

Using the Innovation Climate Questionnaire

You may download and make a few copies of this questionnaire from www.pinchot.com, making sure the Pinchot & Company name, the Internet address, and the copyright information are not deleted. The first five copies are free. You can fill out the questionnaire on-line at www.pinchot.com and receive in return some data on norms. We can also conduct an audit of your climate for innovation.

How to use this chapter

Fill out the questionnaire yourself. What are the major supports and the major barriers to innovation in your organization?

To go a bit deeper, ask a few others in your organization to complete the questionnaire. Get together over lunch or in a conference room and discuss the results. See the end of this chapter for a suggested process to deepen that discussion. In any case, consider these questions:

■ Constructive change begins with recognizing the strengths on which we can build. What strengths does our organization have that would support innovation?
■ What areas have the most room for improvement?
■ Where are the highest-leverage opportunities for improvement— that is, the areas where change would be both most significant and most doable?

THE PINCHOT & COMPANY
INNOVATION CLIMATE QUESTIONNAIRE

What do we mean by "innovation"? Innovation is both the creating and bringing into profitable use of new technologies, new products, new services, new marketing ideas, new systems, and new ways of operating. Implementation is generally the bottleneck that limits the rate of innovation.

This survey consists of both multiple-choice questions and a place at the end to provide textual responses.

1. TRANSMISSION OF VISION AND STRATEGIC INTENT

Employees are more effectively empowered if they are given a clear vision of the future and where the company is trying to go. The need for innovation is then apparent to them, and they know how to direct their efforts.

Check the statements that are more true than false in your organization:
- ❏ Our organizational vision and strategies are clear to me.
- ❏ The vision and strategies would work if applied, but management decisions don't fit with them.
- ❏ The vision and strategies often help me in setting priorities.
- ❏ Strategies are changed so often that no one at my level pays much attention to them.
- ❏ Our organization's announced visions and strategies inspire me.
- ❏ Little effort has been made to clarify what the vision and strategy mean to us in this area.
- ❏ My boss has created a reasonably clear vision and strategy for our area.

2. TOLERANCE OF RISK, MISTAKES, AND FAILURE

Both innovation and organizational learning require trying new things, seeing what happens, and learning from the experience. When those trying new ideas are punished for "mistakes," two things go wrong: (1) people stop experimenting, and (2) mistakes are covered up, so no organizational learning results.

Check the statements that are more true than false in your organization:
❑ Honest and original mistakes are recognized as an indication of initiative and courage.
❑ Even minor mistakes are punished.
❑ Good management of projects involving risk and unpredictability is highly valued, even when things don't turn out according to plan.
❑ New ventures are held to the same standards of predictability as well-established businesses.
❑ Experiments are OK in the lab, but not in the marketplace.
❑ People who make mistakes are encouraged to share them widely so that others can learn.

3. SUPPORT FOR INTRAPRENEURS

Intrapreneurs are employees who behave like entrepreneurs on behalf of the company. They are persistent visionaries who act courageously to turn ideas into profitable realities. They become the hands-on leaders of specific innovations within an organization. Intrapreneurs are an essential ingredient in every successful innovation process.

In your experience, how does your organization respond to intrapreneurs?

Check the statements that are more true than false in your organization:
❑ Effective intrapreneurs are generally rewarded.
❑ We so frustrate people who have the intrapreneurial spirit that most of them leave within their first five years.
❑ Many of our general managers, business unit managers, and directors have a prior history of intrapreneurial success.
❑ Even after success, the first conspicuous failure is a career-limiting event.
❑ I can think of a number of intrapreneurs who have survived and prospered at our organization.
❑ Even when the business results are good, the bold behaviors that lead to intrapreneurial success are punished.

4. MANAGERS WHO SPONSOR INNOVATION

Sponsors are people with power or influence who support, coach, protect, and find resources for an intrapreneurial project and its team.

What percentage of your organization's managers have the skills, power, commitment, and courage to be effective sponsors of intrapreneurial initiatives?
- ❏ 0–5%
- ❏ 6–15%
- ❏ 16–30%
- ❏ 31–50%
- ❏ 51–75%
- ❏ 76–100%

5. EMPOWERED CROSS-FUNCTIONAL TEAMS

Innovative organizations create cross-disciplinary project teams to implement innovation, and they empower them to make decisions. For example, a new product team might—at a minimum—include people from marketing, engineering, and manufacturing.

Check the statements that are more true than false in your organization:
- ❏ Project teams in our organization have considerable freedom to make decisions and act on them without needing to ask for permission.
- ❏ Cross-functional team members come as "ambassadors" from their functional organizations—they negotiate with teammates, but functional bosses who are not part of the team generally make the real decisions.
- ❏ Project teams have considerable choice in recruiting and selecting new team members.
- ❏ We have some effective teams, but most so-called "teams" are really a bunch of individuals with rather different visions of where the project is going.
- ❏ We are using cross-functional teams well.
- ❏ We use teams effectively within functions, but we don't have many effective cross-functional teams or cross-business-unit teams.
- ❏ We rarely use teams effectively; bosses assign work to individuals, not to teams.

6. DECISION MAKING BY THE DOERS

Some organizations push most decisions up to a level way above the doers. Such organizations are not good at implementing innovation.

What percentage of your time is spent getting or waiting for permission to act rather than taking action or gathering information so that you and your team can make your own decisions?
- ❏ 0–10%
- ❏ 11–25%
- ❏ 26–40%
- ❏ 41–65%
- ❏ 66–85%
- ❏ 86–100%

7. DISCRETIONARY TIME

New ideas and hunches require exploration before their value can be demonstrated to others. Innovative organizations give people the freedom to use some of their time to explore new ideas and hunches without having to ask permission.

What percentage of your time at work can you safely divert from your assigned tasks to explore new ideas you believe have promise?
- ❏ 0–2%
- ❏ 3–5%
- ❏ 6–10%
- ❏ 11–20%
- ❏ 21–40%
- ❏ 41–100%

8. ATTENTION ON THE FUTURE

What an organization becomes depends in part on how far ahead it looks. Innovation is more likely to occur when people are thinking well into the future.

In talking with me, my boss's attention rarely extends beyond
- ❏ The next day
- ❏ The next week
- ❏ The next month
- ❏ The next year
- ❏ The next five years
- ❏ The next twenty-five years

9. SELF SELECTION

Intrapreneurs appoint themselves to their roles and then seek the corporation's blessing for their tasks. Intrapreneurial team members are recruited rather than told to join the team. Despite this, some corporations still appoint people to carry out innovations.

Check the statements that are more true than false in your organization:
❑ Most people leading innovation projects are appointed without much concern for whether they are passionate about the idea.
❑ Most people leading innovation projects are self-selected intrapreneurs.
❑ Individuals have considerable influence on the selection of the teams and projects on which they serve.
❑ Team members are recruited by the team leader and may choose whether to join.
❑ Team members are appointed on the basis of availability, not interest, compatibility, or passion for the idea.
❑ It is often very difficult to get permission to leave one's current assignment to join an intrapreneurial team.
❑ If someone wants to join an intrapreneurial team and the team wants him or her, he or she is generally allowed to do so.

10. NO HAND-OFFS

The knowledge generated by an intrapreneurial project is stored in its people. Despite this, when an intrapreneurial project becomes successful, corporations often take it from those who created that success and give it to "professional managers." In general, each early-stage hand-off has a 90 percent chance of killing the project.

Check the statements that are more true than false in your organization:
❑ Our development process includes a series of planned hand-offs from stage to stage.
❑ In theory, we honor the right of intrapreneurs to manage the projects they have created, but in practice, once they succeed, other managers generally take over.
❑ Intrapreneurial leaders and at least half the core team frequently stay with the project from near the beginning to full implementation.

❑ Intrapreneurs and key team members are frequently transferred to other assignments.

❑ We get good team continuity up through the launch of a new product, but around that time, the team often moves on and new people take over.

❑ People come and go in development teams, but there is always a good overlap of project old-timers who maintain memory of the team's past learning.

11. BOUNDARY CROSSING

New ideas generally don't fit the existing organizational pattern. Therefore innovators have to cross boundaries to get help and support. But bureaucratic managers often say no to people from outside their area, just to demonstrate that they are in control.

What percentage of your time and resources is spent helping people outside your area in ways that are not part of your assigned responsibilities?

❑ 0–2%
❑ 3–7%
❑ 8–15%
❑ 16–30%
❑ 31–50%
❑ 51–100%

12. STRONG ORGANIZATIONAL COMMUNITY

In companies with a strong organizational community, people take care of each other and help each other out. They think in terms of the good of the whole rather than just the agenda of their area. Organizational community provides a base of support for innovators and a force to direct freedom toward worthwhile ends.

Check the statements that are more true than false in your organization:
❑ People feel a strong desire to make contributions to this company and to the people in it.

❑ People are very cynical about the company as a whole and are guided by selfish concerns, including concerns for their immediate area.

❑ Many of us are proud to be part of this company.

❏ I feel a sense of community with my unit or function, but not with the company as a whole.

❏ I don't trust this company or the people in it to support me in times of trouble.

❏ When I ask for help in some other part of the company, people there generally say they're too busy.

❏ There are people in the company who always lend a hand, and we honor them regardless of their rank.

❏ People here feel a strong sense of membership and mutual support.

13. FOCUS ON CUSTOMERS

Refocusing on how to better serve customers drives organizations toward productive innovation. Focus on internal politics tends toward conservatism, mistargeted megaprojects, and failure to exploit genuinely superior technology.

When decisions are made in your organization, what percentage of the criteria (implicit or explicit) relates to understanding and better meeting customers' or users' needs, as opposed to satisfying internal politics and defending turf?

❏ 0–5%

❏ 6–20%

❏ 21–35%

❏ 36–65%

❏ 66–85%

❏ 86–100%

14. CHOICE OF INTERNAL SUPPLIERS

When an intrapreneur faces many internal monopolies for essential services and permissions, the chances are that any truly novel project will be stopped. The most innovative companies provide more than one place to go for most things, so intrapreneurs can "wire around" people who are blocking them.

Check the statements that are more true than false in your organization:

❏ There are many internal monopolies in our company; this causes complacency and forces us to use internal service providers that are not up to the highest standards.

❏ Teams often have a choice among several internal suppliers of services such as information management, training, sales, manufacturing, and software engineering.

❏ If we can't get "what we need when we need it" from inside suppliers, we are generally able to go outside to get it.

❏ Choice exists in the informal systems of our organization, but the formal systems are biased toward internal monopolies.

❏ A team with a new product or service will be told what sales force to use, even if the assigned salespeople are not really interested in selling the new offering.

15. MEASUREMENT OF INNOVATION

Innovation is frequently discouraged by the way performance is measured. The most innovative organizations develop measurements that encourage innovation.

In what areas do the current measurement systems of your organization do more to encourage than to discourage innovation?

❏ Incremental innovation
❏ Breakthrough innovation
❏ Process innovation
❏ Product innovation
❏ Marketing and sales innovation
❏ Support group innovation
❏ Technical invention

16. TRANSPARENCY AND TRUTH

Information is useful to an organization only if the people doing the work and making the decisions have it. In the most innovative organizations, information flows freely, both horizontally and vertically.

Check the statements that are more true than false in your organization:

❏ People here tell the truth, even if it is painful or not what someone wants to hear.

❏ The truth is hidden; people say what bosses want to hear.

❏ We hit a good balance between truthfulness and tact.

❏ Information is closely guarded as a political resource.

❏ We share information about customers freely across organizational boundaries.

❑ We share information about technology freely across the boundaries of the organization.

❑ Fear of leaks to competitors keeps us from sharing information with others in the company who might need it.

❑ At least once a month, we get detailed financial reports on our business.

17. GOOD TREATMENT OF PEOPLE

Companies that treat employees well gain a competitive advantage: employees are more loyal, and they have a greater sense of safety, which gives them the courage to innovate.

When you observe managers of this organization making decisions, what do you see?

Check the items that are more rather than less characteristic of your organization:

❑ A tendency to see all people as people, not as cogs in the machine.

❑ Indifference to the effect of decisions on people's lives.

❑ Willingness to take a short-term earnings hit to protect employees' jobs.

❑ Concern for people as long as there is little cost attached.

❑ Genuine concern for employees, backed up by supportive actions.

❑ Rewards for brutality and intimidation.

❑ Real respect for others, even when they are of lower status in the organization.

18. SOCIAL, ENVIRONMENTAL, AND ETHICAL RESPONSIBILITY

Companies with a strong commitment to serving society's needs—to social, environmental, and ethical responsibility—often anticipate external changes and out-innovate their competitors. In addition, they attract a better type of employee, with greater commitment to serving customers and improving the world.

Check the statements that are more true than false in your organization:

❑ We laugh at anyone who talks about ethical responsibilities beyond compliance.

❑ We have a written commitment to ethical priorities beyond what is required by law.

❏ When making decisions, we take social and environmental issues very seriously.

❏ We obey the law in environmental and social issues, but don't work very hard at going beyond what the law requires.

❏ We are sometimes lax in meeting the requirements of social and environmental laws.

19. AVOIDING THE "HOME RUN" PHILOSOPHY

Many organizations value only those innovations that can be confidently projected to add at least 5–10 percent to the bottom line within a few years. For huge companies, such opportunities are rare; aiming for them usually results in very costly failure. The better way to growth involves numerous smaller bets, many of which succeed modestly and some of which then open the door to huge opportunities in which you have a commanding advantage. Then you may prudently invest for the "home run."

Check the statements that are more true than false in your organization.

❏ Small beginnings are out of favor. We only want home runs.

❏ We are good at managing many small businesses in a decentralized way, so we have many small beginnings in many different places.

❏ Innovation is managed centrally to make sure we invest only in things with the highest potential.

❏ Our desire to promise "big results" fast causes many managers to make mistakes on a larger scale than necessary.

❏ We are good at trying things on a small scale to find out what works.

❏ Once something is shown to work on a small scale, we are good at scaling up quickly.

OPEN-ENDED QUESTIONS

In your experience of your organization, what do you think has been most supportive of innovation?

In your experience of your organization, what has done the most to slow down or stop innovation?

Thank you for participating in this survey.

CHAPTER 13

IMPROVING YOUR CLIMATE FOR INNOVATION

A<small>T EVERY LEVEL</small> of the organization, it is the job of leaders to create the conditions that bring about innovation. This chapter presents ways to strengthen each of the Innovation Success Factors covered in Chapter 12. In each case, we suggest both traditional methods of improvement and methods that stretch traditional ways of thinking. Do not be concerned if some of the stretch solutions are described so briefly that you don't quite grasp them. Most of those we thought might require elaboration are accompanied by references for further reading.

1. TRANSMITTING VISION AND STRATEGIC INTENT

It's not enough that leaders know where their organization should be going. For the vision to have effect, the people of the organization must be moved by the vision. They must understand what they can do to bring it to realization. When they are thus motivated, they can be given considerable freedom without concern that the organization might veer off course.

What should you do if the vision isn't calling forth the kind of directed energy you had hoped for? Here are some solutions that have been successful in other organizations.

Solutions

A. Create a vision that speaks to people's deepest values. (This classic never goes out of style.) Find out what they care about. Probe deeply in your own soul. Discover what is important to you. Consider what is meaningful to customers, and what could be meaningful to them in the future. Ask yourself how the organization addresses society's real needs. Learn what the organization is and could be good at. How do all these things fit together? What vision of its future could lead the organization to be all it could be?

B. Look for visions that are relevant at all levels, from the spiritual to the most practical.

C. Get input from people throughout the organization.

D. Share the evolving vision incessantly. Openly use it to make important decisions.

E. Boldly articulate challenging but achievable qualitative intents and quantitative goals that mark progress toward the vision.

F. Actively enlist the help of those responsible for execution.

Stretch solutions

A. Let all employees participate in the creation and elaboration of the vision. True participation in shaping the vision is the golden path to commitment. This clearly works in the best teams, where the vision is a co-creation of all the members. Good team leaders know how to incorporate other people's ideas as the vision evolves. But can a leader encourage participation when employees number in the thousands? Yes! See stretch solution D below.

B. Align the organization's aspirations with deeper values that give meaning to the work beyond making money.

C. As Motorola does, set some 10x targets—performance goals that call for a measurable tenfold improvement in some performance indicator within a certain period of time.

D. We live at a time of breakthrough in democratic process. Many large-group facilitators today can handle vision-finding and planning retreats with thousands of participants. The visions that emerge often surprise leaders. They had never guessed that their people had such foresight or the courage to set such bodacious goals. Furthermore, the vision created by the whole group is often a strategically astute response to market and technical realities that are more clearly seen by those close to the action. Best of all, the participants who created the vision understand it and are committed to making it work.

E. Can we go further in the direction of participation than even large-scale visioning events? Yes again. The near future will see software that helps people pass visions up and down the organization for feedback, new specificity, new facts, and voluntary alignment with the fundamental intent of the vision. People "below" will work on what the vision means in their area.

As the proposed vision spreads to all parts of the organization, each group can be expected to identify:

- The aspects of the overall vision that give meaning and direction to its existing work.
- The new initiatives sparked by the vision. It will become clear at the local level which of these make good business sense.
- The parts of the proposed vision that might block or invalidate something the group is currently doing, and the costs of not doing it. A good vision has "teeth." It bites existing projects, businesses, functions, and ways of thinking, as well as competitors. A vision is not specific enough unless it implies stopping as well as starting activities. What will be lost if an activity is halted? Is the freeing up of resources worth the loss? Should the vision be modified so that a valuable activity is saved? How?
- An integrated local vision for the group's future role, objectives, and output. This will show how the purpose and focus of the group's activities would change to fit the proposed larger vision.

Dialogue up and down the organization around these issues will hone the vision and make everyone think more clearly about the implications of their work. Senior leaders can strengthen whatever engenders the desired responses and eliminate those elements that threaten to be counterproductive. And they can thank many more people for their help in getting the vision right.

EXTRA POINT

It helps if a vision is held steady over time so that projects inspired by that vision can be completed before it is changed. Define your vision around fundamentals that have lasting value.

2. TOLERANCE OF RISK, MISTAKES, AND FAILURE

In too many organizations, one mistake offsets many successes. What can you do if your organizational culture is hard on even the most sensible of risk takers?

SOLUTIONS

A. Scatter risk-friendly slogans in everything from speeches to bumper stickers. Samples:
If you're not making mistakes, you're probably not doing anything.
Make your mistakes faster and cheaper.
We recover faster from mistakes than from standing still.
B. Use the word *risk* sparingly, as people tend to hear it as a signal of personal danger. Instead, talk about trying things out, conducting experiments, and learning from what happens. Make learning more important than always being right.
C. When trouble strikes, focus on figuring out how to resolve the problem, not on tracking down the culprit. Don't tolerate finger pointing.
D. Desensitize fear of mistakes. Have senior management boast to the troops about the mistakes they have made.
E. Give honorable innovation failures a Noble Attempt Award, and make sure the team's next assignments are good ones.
F. Clearly distinguish between original mistakes made in the course of trying something new and past mistakes repeated out of carelessness. Don't hold innovative projects to the same standards as well-established businesses and mature processes.

STRETCH SOLUTIONS

A. Let successful intrapreneurs earn *intracapital*—a reward for success in the form of a budget they may spend on their next idea without asking anyone for permission. Essentially, it's a bank account for new projects, new equipment, or self-improvement. Successful intrapreneurs are thus empowered to launch new projects without prior approval, and, at least in theory, are immunized against reprimand if the project fails. This device puts some of the company's "risk money" into the hands of proven innovators, who on average are more canny about early-stage investments than executives whose highest skill is managing more mature businesses. (See *Intrapreneuring*, Chapter II.)

B. Provide organizational spaces in which to hide projects. Just as certain species of tropical fish need hiding places in their tanks if they are to breed, so intrapreneurs often will not pursue the mistake-intensive early stages of innovation under the spotlight. Let good sponsors hide early-stage projects. For example,

- Eliminate senior management access to project time reporting on smaller projects.
- Let local managers report progress on successes and bury the failures quietly.
- Learn to observe the details of how your organization functions without having to intervene in the specifics (unless you spot instances of poor ethics, bad character, or company-risking error.) Intervene by changing the force fields that drove local managers to make mistakes, not by getting them in trouble for attracting the attention of the big boss.

3. SUPPORT FOR INTRAPRENEURS

Intrapreneurs are the engines of innovation. If the system doesn't work for them, innovation will slow to a crawl. What can you do if intrapreneurs are not being supported in your organization?

SOLUTIONS

A. Effective, courageous sponsors are the mainstays of any system for supporting intrapreneurs. First, be a sponsor. Second, see the suggestions under "Managers who sponsor innovation," on the next page.

B. Deal with the most important of the other Innovation Success Factors. They all affect intrapreneurs.

C. Run an intraprise start-up workshop as described in Chapter 4.

D. Recognize intrapreneurial teams that succeed! Establish something like 3M's Golden Steps award for new product teams that achieve a certain level of sales in a short period of time. 3M gives each member of the team a sculpture of Mercury's winged feet commemorating the success. The awards bestow great status and can later be used to intimidate fussbudget bureaucrats who are exercising their power to say no.

E. Create a financial reward system appropriate to intrapreneurs. (See *Intrapreneuring*, 260–299.)

F. Whenever you hear about a successful innovation, visit the team and give each member five personally signed Free Blooper Cards. These cards say:

> Please excuse [person's name]'s mistake. He[/She] has earned the right to make a bunch of 'em at our expense.
> Thanks,
> [Your signature]

G. Find out who the intrapreneurs in your organization are. Get them together in a meeting with a good outside facilitator. Ask them what needs to be done to make the system work for intrapreneurs.

STRETCH SOLUTION

Establish a free intraprise system. (See Chapter 14; also, *The Intelligent Organization*, 131–191.)

4. MANAGERS WHO SPONSOR INNOVATION

Sponsors can help intrapreneurs cut through the red tape and non-constructive politics that exist in all of today's organizations. Even if there is a lot wrong with your company's climate for innovation, you will still get effective intrapreneuring, and thus cost-effective innovation, if there are enough good sponsors. For this reason, would-be climate makers should put lots of attention on giving managers the motivation, the power, and the skills to be effective sponsors of intrapreneurial initiatives.

SOLUTIONS

A. Be an effective sponsor yourself. An effective sponsor calms the immune system and deflects its tendency to see the intrapreneur as a foreign body to be attacked. As both a coach and a behind-the-scenes advocate, he or she helps intrapreneurs both to avoid trouble and to get resources.

B. Make sponsorship an essential part of the desired profile of a leader. Promote sponsors, not bureaucrats or hatchet men.

C. Have human resources make a list of the most effective sponsors by asking the company's intrapreneurs, "In your darkest hour on that project, who defended you and gave you the advice you needed to survive?" Keep this list a top-secret part of the succession planning process, because often a sponsor revealed is a sponsor disempowered. Great sponsors get results by letting others take credit, so let those late on the bandwagon receive the kudos. But the next time a promotion is on the table, consult the real sponsors list.

D. Ask the intrapreneurs you run into who were the most effective sponsors in the early stages of their innovation. Send each sponsor a note saying: "I hear you are a great sponsor. Let me know how I can back you up." Also see that good sponsors are well represented in succession planning documents.

STRETCH SOLUTIONS

A. Train *all* managers in the role of sponsor.

B. Once a free intraprise system is established (see Chapter 14), let sponsors use their own intracapital to buy shares in intraprises. The best of them will acquire more intracapital and become, in effect, internal venture capitalists. The result will be a more creative and more effective free intraprise system.

5. EMPOWERED CROSS-FUNCTIONAL TEAMS

Avoid "The Ambassador Syndrome," which occurs when a team essentially consists of ambassadors from hostile functions, representing the wishes of their masters, rather than genuine team members working together to find and implement the right answer. When team members' primary loyalty is to their "home" function rather than to the cross-functional team, attention tends to be focused on departmental priorities and functional niceties rather than on achieving the mission. The process slows to a crawl and, in the end, the customer is not served.

When work is done in empowered cross-functional teams, members' primary loyalty is to the success of the project and the team. The focus shifts to the customer. Decisions are made on the basis of what will win the customer's business and make money for the company, not on what makes life easier for one of the functions at the expense of the whole.

SOLUTIONS

A. Create product development—and process innovation—systems in which work is done holistically in strong cross-functional teams rather than piecemeal by different functions that don't communicate.

B. Give more power to the project leader and the team and less to the functional managers to whom the team members report. Functional managers will no longer be allocating and controlling employees. Their job will be (1) to educate and develop their staff; (2) to market them to project team leaders; and (3) to research, evolve, and maintain tools and standards of functional excellence. The team leader and the team are responsible for project results and most project-related decisions.

C. Create an informal culture in which team members and sponsors can go to their colleagues and get what they need without a lot of red tape.

D. Make sure that, at appraisal time, functional managers are given credit when their people make good contributions to cross-functional teams.

STRETCH SOLUTION

Let intrapreneurial teams select a board of sponsors that will govern major policy and investment decisions and otherwise help the team get the resources and "space" it needs to manage its own destiny.

- Give the team a budget and let it make decisions within the limits set. For new businesses and products, the budget should limit cumulative losses, not expenditures. Revenue earned adds to the budget.
- When a board-level decision is needed, the board of sponsors must be willing to come together quickly or to make the decision with a number of members missing. Use conference calls and e-mail voting.
- Remove members of the board who don't have time to work on the team's behalf.

6. DECISION MAKING BY THE DOERS

The essence of effective innovation is finding talented intrapreneurs with the passion to go in the right general direction, providing them with the necessary resources, keeping them on track with tough questions and a bit of advice, and above all, *letting them get on with it.* This means trusting them and, beyond advice and protection, intervening only if they are doing something that puts the larger organization in significant danger. It means building systems in which innovators spend more time innovating than they do getting permissions, begging for resources, and writing reports.

SOLUTIONS

A. Create a task force to identify and remove unnecessary controls. Ask employees at all levels what forms, sign-offs, procedures, reports, approvals, and reviews appear to be excessive or unnecessary. Find out who believes they are useful. Eliminate all the controls that lack strong champions, all the reports that nobody really reads. Then begin questioning the cost-effectiveness of the rest. Make control freaks accountable for the cost and time consumption of the systems they impose on others.

B. Establish one or more seed money funds, perhaps along the lines of DuPont's $eed Fund or 3M's Alpha and Genesis programs. Seed money funds give employees another place to go, outside their normal chain of command, for permission and resources. This quickly unjams the front end of the innovation system.

One plan: appoint a relatively low-level committee—sprinkled with innovators—and empower it to hand out grants of $1,000 to $50,000 (the range depending on the size of the company) to research or try out an idea. The money will generally help the innovator take the first step toward proof of concept, after which she will have to reenter the normal approval channels. Our experience with seed funds is that within three years they generally have earned a measured return of ten times the amount originally invested.

C. Allow managers to get discretionary funds by canceling or cutting back budgeted projects and reusing the money saved in new ones.

D. Use sponsors to negotiate behind the scenes to clear the path for intrapreneurs and their teams.

E. Create an "It's all right to say you don't know" culture. If managers are expected to know everything their people are doing all the time, the culture is not one of trust and empowerment.

STRETCH SOLUTIONS

A. Hold divisions responsible for creating innovations, both the kind that are useful within their existing lines of business and the kinds that move into the white spaces between businesses. This gives each division motivation to expand its people's freedom of operation.

B. Build uncommitted funds into budgets and push discretion to spend them further down in the organization. This is not additional spending. Approve fewer projects and leave 10 percent uncommitted for what may come up later.

C. Create a free intraprise system with multiple sources of internal risk capital. Most of these sources should be in the hands of proven intrapreneurs and proven sponsors. For more information, see Chapter 14 and *The Intelligent Organization,* Chapters 6, 7, 8, and 9; also download articles on free intraprise from the books and articles section of the Pinchot & Company website, www.pinchot.com.

D. Each time you put a new system in place, consider its erosive effect on managers' power to make decisions. Restore the power to lead and support innovation at middle and lower levels. When left alone, bureaucracy nibbles away at freedom until little is left.

E. Create an intracapital bank. The bank is an internal accounting system that provides banking services to intrapreneurial enterprises or "intraprises." The bank becomes a vehicle for granting a specified financial authority to the intraprise team. A sponsor can deposit funds that the team then uses to buy supplies and to pay for services, thereby circumventing normal approval channels. The team's revenues also are deposited in the intracapital bank, and over time it earns increasing freedom from bosses as long as it continues to live within its means. See *The Intelligent Organization,* 155–160, for more on how such a system works.

F. Create internal service intraprises—teams that sell their services to other parts of the organization and are profit centers with accounts in the intracapital bank. (See the U.S. Forest Service reinvention lab case in Chapter 4.)

Internal service intraprises liberate both the teams that provide services and their customers. Because they move across boundaries to serve customers, these enterprises act as powerful conduits for cross-organizational transfer of best practices. Customers are liberated from bureaucratic suppliers as a result of having choice. Intrapreneurial suppliers of services are liberated from their bureaucratic bosses because, if they are good enough at what they do, they need take on only those customers they enjoy working with. In competing to win customers, they also produce breakthroughs in "staff" efficiency. Use internal service intraprises to build the infrastructure that will liberate all kinds of intrapreneurial teams.

7. DISCRETIONARY TIME

Most intrapreneurial innovation begins somewhere near the bottom of the organization, where most of the people are. Ideas not watered with action soon wilt and die. If no time can be pried loose to try something new, very little intrapreneuring will take place. How can you put a little "bootleg slack" into the system so that new ideas can be tried out and information gathered before subjecting them to a formal approval process many levels removed from where the intrapreneurs live?

SOLUTIONS

A. Announce a 10 or 15 percent rule: all exempt employees (those not eligible for overtime pay) get 10 or 15 percent of their time to work on projects of their own choosing. Let them use that time as they see fit, as long as the projects are for the benefit of the organization or its customers. Don't chide them for their choices. Companies as diverse as IBM, DuPont, and 3M use the 10 percent rule in some part of their organization.

B. Reduce the number of mandated projects to fit the available human resources. Don't assign more work than can possibly be done.

C. Value people who stop to investigate a new idea or an unexplained phenomenon.

D. Value results, not the appearance of continuous effort.

STRETCH SOLUTIONS

A. Allow people to choose which project teams they want to work on. Use this as a way of reducing the total number of projects. If no one wants to work on a project, treat this as important feedback and strongly consider eliminating it.

B. Give teams more control over how their work gets done. Let them schedule themselves so that they can cover for a member who needs time to check out a new idea.

C. Charge for staff services. There will always be excess demand and long queues for good staff services as long as the incremental cost to users is zero. When people use only what is cost-effective, staff has more time for innovation.

8. ATTENTION ON THE FUTURE

Innovation takes time, but the rhythm of corporations is determined by quarterly profits. Can the company decide to try something and stick with it through the inevitable learning process, with all its mistakes and false starts? Is there a source of what venture capitalists call "patient money"?

SOLUTIONS

A. Involve large numbers of people in visioning exercises that look five, ten, and fifty years into the future.
B. In every meeting, bring up the effect of decisions on the organization two to ten years into the future. Notice who cares and who considers it silly.
C. Put long-term thinking into appraisals.

STRETCH SOLUTIONS

A. Hire and promote people who take a longer view. Keep people with close time horizons at lower levels of the organization. (See Elliott Jaques, *A General Theory of Bureaucracy.*[5])
B. Appraise people on longer cycles. What is the present effect of the management they did five years ago? For example, what did they sponsor five and ten years ago, and how did it turn out?

9. SELF-SELECTION

The best intrapreneurial teams consist of volunteers. Innovative organizations value volunteer energy and look for intrapreneurs already in motion. They allow the volunteer team to "own" the project once it becomes official.

SOLUTIONS

A. Allow professionals to choose which teams to join.
B. Allow teams and their leaders to decide which members to accept.
C. Do not force growing intrapreneurial businesses to accept as team members people who are having difficulty finding jobs elsewhere in the organization.

Stretch solutions

A. Incorporate the three solutions above in the organization's written policies.
B. If that is too radical, give members of an honor society made up of successful innovators the formal right to choose which teams to join, and their teams the right to choose members.
C. Institute an intrapreneurial bill of rights. (See Appendix F.)
D. Create a judicial body that employees can go to when their intrapreneurial rights are violated.
E. Discipline any manager who attempts to violate employees' intrapreneurial rights.

10. No hand-offs

As the intrapreneurial team blunders through the early stages of innovation, the major value created is learning what works and what does not in the area of the intraprise. If the project is handed off to other people, much of that learning is lost. The best innovation processes let the core team of committed intrapreneurs stay with the project from beginning to well past commercial success. Good managers of innovation will resist the temptation to remove the "untested" intrapreneurs who have just created the business and replace them with less intrapreneurial but politically well-connected "professional" managers.

Solutions

A. Whenever possible, let intrapreneurs stay with their projects from beginning to end.
B. If changes in the team have to be made, move team members one at a time. Keep the team memory intact by overlapping tenures.
C. Allow intrapreneurial teams to recruit members, and make it difficult for other managers to prevent recruits from joining a team if they wish to do so. Obviously, they must give reasonable notice and complete their previous projects in such a way that others can take over.

Stretch solutions

A. Give employees the *right* to develop and grow their creations. This applies not only to inventors but also to the intrapreneurial team that takes the innovation from idea to business reality. Require a difficult due process before others can take over the fruits of a team's labor without its permission.

B. Remove intrapreneurial leaders only when their teams no longer trust them, not when they have begun to annoy bureaucrats or arouse the jealousy of empire builders.

11. BOUNDARY CROSSING

Innovation almost always crosses the boundaries of the organization because those boundaries, quite properly, reflect the current way of running the existing business. Bureaucratic organizations often have a culture that supports extreme behavior in the defense of one's turf. Turf-conscious managers say no to people from outside their area just to demonstrate that they are in control. How do you build a culture that honors generosity across boundaries, not territorial defense? (For related solutions, see also "Organizational community" and "Focus on customers" on pages 131 and 132.)

SOLUTIONS

A. Encourage people to create a boundaryless organization. (This does not always work.)

B. Create a culture that trades favors across boundaries—"One hand washes the other." (This works, but suffers the limitations of barter economies.)

C. Rotate people across boundaries so that they better understand each other. (This works, but if the rotation is too rapid, no one learns from mistakes and the company only gets information on short-term performance and style. Corporations with rapid rotation of "high potentials" tend to promote people who merely talk a good game and have a very limited time horizon. Staying in one place is a good way to learn wisdom by cleaning up one's own mistakes. Furthermore, rapid rotation works against "No hand-offs.")

D. Find a high-level sponsor who presides over both sides of the boundary. (This may be practical in a specific situation, but it is generally inadequate for creating a system with high capacity for innovation. Unfortunately, people at high levels still have only two ears and twenty-four hours in the day.)

E. Throw a party and invite the other side in a cross-boundary conflict in for food and drink.

F. Exchange gifts—do something to support the other side's projects.

G. Thank people for their help.

H. Encourage cooperation low in the hierarchy. People at lower levels are often less turf-conscious than their bosses, whose incentives may dictate a division-only focus.

I. Reward whole-company performance—for example, through profit sharing and employee ownership.

STRETCH SOLUTIONS

A. Assess generosity across boundaries in all appraisals.

B. Make cross-boundary contributions visible. For example, create a central site to which one can report acts of cross-boundary generosity and information sharing.

C. Build organizational community. See *The Community of the Future,*[6] issued by the Drucker Foundation. Also, visit the books and articles section of www.pinchot.com and download articles on organizational community.

D. Use the free intraprise system for internal services. This will bring into being and fund teams that live by carrying information across boundaries.

12. STRONG ORGANIZATIONAL COMMUNITY

When people in organizations stop helping each other out across boundaries, it is plain that the sense of organizational community is breaking down. The cause may be chronic overwork and time pressures, an excessive focus on the chain of command, or lack of the kind of leadership that builds community. At the heart of community are people caring for the whole and for fellow members. The principle that builds community is respect for those who contribute to the community and its members, not for those who have power over it or who take the most from it. Great leaders earn respect—and expect their subordinates to earn respect—by contributing, not by instilling fear.

SOLUTIONS

A. Choose great leaders who will inspire people to unite behind a worthwhile common purpose. (Certainly the simplest solution, but often hard to execute.)

B. Co-create a defined set of values that will actually govern behavior. Shared values build community.

c. Build a culture that takes care of its members. Extreme examples: a guarantee of lifetime employment; the Marine Corps' commitment to bring back its wounded and dead from the battlefield.

D. As much as possible, work toward greater equality. Inequalities of rank, privilege, and power erode community spirit. Avoid symbols of rank, excessive pay differences, and a domineering style of management.

E. Celebrate anyone's success as a win for all members.

STRETCH SOLUTIONS

A. Build a widespread appreciation of the gift economy, which is the economic basis of community. The gift economy follows rules quite different from those used in the exchange economy with which we are all so familiar. (See *The Gift: Imagination and the Erotic Life of Property,* by Lewis Hyde.[7]) In an exchange economy, the one who gets more is considered the winner. In the gift economy, status comes not from what you get or have but rather from what you give. For example, a professor's status is not based on his or her salary, but rather on the quality and quantity of published contributions to the field. One need not view this giving as unselfish. Consider two professors who attend a conference. One of them sleeps through many of the sessions and takes away little new knowledge. In fact, she is forgetful and is not a fount of knowledge about all aspects of her field. However, she gives a paper that will be quoted by all attendees. The other professor, who has an encyclopedic knowledge of the field, absorbs everything at the conference but gives no papers. Whose status is higher? In academia, having or getting knowledge confers only minor status. One gets status by contributing knowledge to one's field. This is the gift economy, and the rules are almost the opposite of the exchange economy in which "he who dies with the most toys wins." Within your organization, build up a parallel system in which status is based on appreciation of what people contribute rather than the more conventional respect for power, position, and wealth. (See *The Intelligent Organization,* Chapter 11, and the books and articles section of www.pinchot.com for further information on the gift economy.)

B. The military has long used medals as symbols of honor for contributions above and beyond the call of duty. How can you introduce something analogous to medals within the context of your culture?

The e-mail system at Sun Microsystems has little figures called avatars that represent senders. As a person contributes more to Sun, he gets to add hats and clothes to his avatar, which represent the status he has achieved with his contributions.

C. Reward those who give generously of their time to other members of the organizational community or to projects valuable to the organization as a whole.

13. FOCUS ON CUSTOMERS

A focus on customers redirects people's attention from pleasing bosses and defending turf to collaborating on ways to get the customers what they need at a price and quality that will win their business. How do you get people to focus on customers?

SOLUTIONS

A. Send all types of employees to spend time with customers.
B. Arrange for designers to observe the customer at close hand. Example: a calculator design engineer spent six months as a calculator salesperson. That's getting close to your customer!
C. Measure customer satisfaction and make it a key to advancement and bonuses.
D. Assign each senior executive a specific customer to care for.
E. Build a customer-focused organization around value propositions.

STRETCH SOLUTIONS

A. Send out whole teams to spend time with customers as they work. Example: a team developing electronics for police squad cars spent many nights on the road with the police. Team members witnessed multiple arrests and even found themselves in the middle of a shoot-out. They came back with a much better understanding of police officers' true needs and preferences. Their designs and market positioning changed radically.
B. Establish a free intraprise system. This will focus all support functions on providing service to those who directly serve the firm's customers.

14. CHOICE OF INTERNAL SUPPLIERS

Entrepreneurs live in a multi-option world. If one supplier does not meet their needs quickly and efficiently, they can go to another. This system breeds efficiency, innovation, and high-quality service. Intrapreneurs, by contrast, too often face internal monopoly suppliers of both permission and essential resources and services. Only one sales force may be designated to sell their product or one function to produce the packaging. If a person of power within one of those monopoly suppliers decides not to support the intrapreneur, there may be no recourse except to try to go over that individual's head. A system that includes many essential monopolies frustrates innovation. How can you design systems that offer multiple options?

SOLUTIONS

A. Allow divisions to go outside the organization for some services that can also be bought inside. (But for a warning on the overuse of outsourcing, see *The Intelligent Organization,* Chapter 9.)
B. Convert allocated staff *services* to charge-backs and give people choice over what to buy from those service providers. Distinguish between staff services and other staff activities:

- Is this a service to identifiable internal customers in operating divisions?
- Is this a service to the corporate office?
- Is this a police, inspection, or regulating activity?

Charge internal customers only for services they use voluntarily. Bill the other two categories (services to the corporate office and policing) to corporate and maintain them as part of a modest allocated overhead.

Don't allow one group to both regulate and sell services to the same customer. Put regulation and the provision of services to meet the regulations into two separate organizational units.

It is often acceptable for a group to provide services to both divisional and corporate clients. And mixing services to the corporate office with policing of the divisions can work. But never mix service to the divisions with divisional policing. That leads to the trading of "protection"—for example: "Buy my consulting service and

I can guarantee you will pass inspection, because I'm the inspector. Fail to buy and . . . ."

c. Allow multiple providers of service to evolve naturally. If one division has a staff group that sells services to another division, do not let the corporate staff for that function block, suppress, or incorporate the divisional service provider. Let them remain in business as an additional provider that other divisions can turn to if they want. Multiple options arise naturally as long as they are not prohibited by a corporate prejudice against "redundancy." If the divisional staff group competes with the corporate group for internal customers, may the best provider win.

d. Streamline internal billing for services so that it is very easy for one division to sell services to another and get paid with money that is subtracted from the budget of the buyer and added to the budget of the seller.

Stretch solution

Establish a full-blown free intraprise system in which teams of intrapreneurs sell their services to other parts of the organization. The basic steps are:

- Create quick and easy systems for setting up intraprises, especially those serving internal customers.
- Establish institutions for defining and registering joint ownership of an intraprise so that team members can own shares in their intraprises.
- Put in place a fast and efficient internal justice system, with fair courts and judges, to which disputes can be taken.
- Formulate intraproperty rights and empower the justice system to make sure no one ignores them.
- Create an intracapital bank to clear transfer payments and to serve as a depository for intracapital.
- Allow every intraprise to establish an account, deposit receipts, and write "checks" to other parts of the organization. Solve the associated accounting problems.
- Set up a system for registering agreements and contracts. Make sure everyone treats promises with great respect. This means not only keeping commitments but allowing those below you to keep their commitments to others as well.

■ Design an effective process for rapidly establishing a body of internal "commercial law." Use the larger society's commercial law as a conceptual starting point, but seek simpler and faster procedures. Build a low-friction internal economy.

■ Promote worker ownership of the whole organization to increase cross-system cooperation.

(Adapted from *The Intelligent Organization,* page 149; for more detail, see Chapters 6–9 of that book. Also, visit the books and articles section of www.pinchot.com and look for articles about free intraprise.)

15. MEASUREMENT OF INNOVATION

People in large organizations often complain that most measurements discourage innovations that take more than a short time to pay off. The problem is that measurements can only look backward, not forward. But that is a fact of nature, not an organizational flaw. What can you do to make measurement an ally of innovation?

Solutions

A. Compute the percentage of your organization's products that were introduced in the latest relevant time period (six months to five years, depending on the product life cycle of the industry).

B. Measure the length of the new product cycle.

C. Measure the rate of cost reduction.

D. Count the number of patents.

E. Measure quality improvements (reduced variation and errors).

F. Measure growth rate.

G. Count process innovations.

H. Measure new markets and market segments engaged.

Stretch solutions

A. Measure the quality and quantity of innovation. 3M takes both measures in each of its divisions and holds managers responsible for them, as well as for the better-publicized "percent of products new in the last three years." Quality is measured according to defined criteria, but the judgments are still subjective, and for the sake of fairness, are made by a traveling innovation evaluation team.

B. When categorizing innovations, ask, Does this innovation create a "new gene" that can spawn many new products and services, or is it merely a good step forward in an already established direction?

C. Let the users of staff services choose between internal providers in a free intraprise system. The more innovative providers will find ways to deliver better and more cost-effective services. Therefore customers' willingness to buy when they have choice is probably a less political and more accurate measure of innovation in providing services than any committee report on "innovativeness." A system in which buyers have choice will generally reward innovation.

D. Compare your price with your competitors' prices. If you can charge higher prices than your competitors and keep your customers, either you have created superior products or you have innovative marketing.

16. TRANSPARENCY AND TRUTH

Healthy organizations provide for rapid, accurate feedback. Such feedback is available only if people tell the truth and are willing to hear it.

SOLUTIONS

A. Demand, as Jack Welch does at General Electric, that people "face reality and communicate candidly." Welch fires those who beat around the bush or tell him only what he wants to hear.

B. Create an open-book company. Provide copious information to all employees, including weekly financials. (See Jack Stack and Bo Burlingham, *The Great Game of Business*[8]; also John Schuster, Jill Carpenter with M. Patricia Kane, *The Power of Open-Book Management*.[9]

C. Model openness and insist that all your managers do so, too. Be intolerant of people who guard information as a political resource.

D. Distinguish between commands, which flow along defined lines, and information, which should flow freely wherever needed. Be very severe with leaders who discipline their people for passing on information to others within the company.

E. Don't shoot the messenger, and don't let others do it.

F. Promote and otherwise honor the truth tellers, even if they are a bit unsettling at times. Reward those who make waves by telling the truth.

Stretch solution

Look for ways to make freedom of speech a right in your organization. Advanced societies work better with freedom of speech and freedom of the press. The same is surely true of advanced corporations, but we have a long way to go in that direction. For a preliminary exploration of these ideas, see *The Intelligent Organization,* Chapter 5.

17. Good treatment of people

People take more risks when coming from a safe base. Those in brutal companies seek safe places to hide, not opportunities to innovate. Such companies see their best talent migrate elsewhere. How can you create an organization that treats people well?

Solutions

A. Make rules about how people are to be treated and insist that managers follow the rules. (Not a good idea if seen as the main solution.)

B. List principles to follow in the treatment of people. Principles do more to define a culture than rules, especially when they are developed with input from all and adhered to by those at the top.

C. Don't reward brutal behavior, even when it produces good short-term results.

D. Create a safety net for employees who lose their job in one part of the organization. Work hard to help them find a place elsewhere within the organization, but don't force them on anyone. Agree to take them back into "special assignment" if the group you place them with doesn't want to keep them. Make it easy to move people out of an intrapreneurial unit where they are not effective by providing lots of help with retraining and reassignment. Give people who have been with the organization for some time but have performed poorly several opportunities to redeem themselves before firing them from the larger organization. A good safety net helps to build organizational community, increases people's willingness to take risks, facilitates the movement of employees out of places where they are not using their highest talents, and encourages teams to evolve toward 100 percent functionality.

E. Measure and care deeply about staff retention. Do careful exit interviews and listen deeply to what people say. Check into the truth of it.

STRETCH SOLUTIONS

A. Create and implement a bill of rights for employees. (See Appendix F and *The Intelligent Organization,* 364–365.)

B. Focus more on the upside—not on how you can avoid treating people badly but on what you can do to make working in your organization a great experience.

C. Regardless of how good their financial results may be, get rid of managers who treat people badly. However, make sure that you look searchingly at grievances and balance the good with the bad. Don't fire a manager who is generally respected by his or her people just because a few of them claim to be victims. Punishing managers for complaints may motivate them to let people get away with all kinds of lapses and abuses.

D. Ask the CEO to do exit interviews, urging him or her to listen deeply and compassionately to what people have to say. If the company is large, the CEO could do every tenth or every hundredth exit interview.

18. SOCIAL, ENVIRONMENTAL, AND ETHICAL RESPONSIBILITY

Today, the best talent is rarely willing to work for money alone. People need to feel that their work will result in something worthwhile. This desire to make a significant difference is also the impulse that drives intrapreneuring. Those who are talented enough to have their pick of employers will gravitate toward companies that have high social, environmental, and ethical standards.

When people with lots of talent find themselves in companies of questionable responsibility, most find that their heart is no longer in their work. They may still come to work, but they are not likely to become intrapreneurs or make any other extraordinary contribution. Such companies are losing the innovation game to those who have figured out the new rules of the talent economy.

To see how strong ethical stands can be significant business assets, study Henkel's industry-shifting move to nonphosphate detergents, DuPont's government lobbying for faster phase out of CFCs, and The Body Shop's retention of staff through community service and support for worthwhile causes.

SOLUTIONS

A. Create staff groups to police environmental compliance.
B. Ensure that the public affairs department contributes to worthwhile organizations in the larger community.
C. Make it very clear in word and deed that the organization is dead serious about its posted values and operating principles.
D. Have a written commitment to social, ethical, and environmental performance well beyond what is required by law.
E. Get out ahead of regulation and celebrate the savings when you don't have to retrofit your systems.

STRETCH SOLUTION

Creating a company committed to the highest social, ethical, and environmental standards is not a matter of tricks and programs. It requires committed, courageous, and competent leadership. Those who claim higher ground will be judged harshly when they fall short of their aspirations, and yet you must talk about the quest if you are going to involve employees. Aim high and be humble about your progress to date.

19. AVOIDING THE "HOME RUN" PHILOSOPHY

When organizations become concerned about innovation, they often put in place a system focused on hitting "innovation home runs." They believe that lots of smaller successes cannot solve their problems, so they set off to find the Holy Grail. All too often, this strategy ends in disaster. Why?

■ It is very hard to tell which innovations will evolve into home runs. For one of our clients, we examined fifteen-year-old strategic evaluations of the potential of a number of projects. We compared those evaluations with the later results. There was a strong relationship between the items deemed to be strategic and later success, but the relationship was negative! Nearly all the projects dubbed "strategic" failed. Many of those dubbed "low potential" became huge businesses that the company is very glad to have today. If it's really hard to pick the big winners, focusing on a few large projects is a dangerous strategy.

▣ By focusing all innovation resources on a few big projects, companies kill off the intrapreneurial spirit everywhere else. There are no intrapreneurs training on smaller projects. Most would-be innovators get frustrated and leave.

▣ The vast majority of innovations, even those destined to become large-scale, begin small. At first, their ultimate uses are not even imagined. Radio was originally used for ship-to-shore communications; broadcasting wasn't considered. Most breakthrough innovations should remain small enterprises until they have blundered their way to some pattern of successes. They make their errors on a small and inexpensive scale and don't wear out their welcome with catastrophic mistakes.

▣ If you invest in home run proportions on an early idea, you risk such heavy losses that there will be no second chance. If you invest lightly in small beginnings and then heavily only in ideas that have begun to succeed and have uncovered a large underserved market, your chances of a good return are far greater.

▣ The success percentage is higher on small innovation efforts, because they attract less determined competition. But the reasons for higher ROI go beyond that. Some small beginnings blossom into large investment opportunities that are low risk and at the same time have a very high return. The significant risk has been taken at the start. Once the idea proves out, scaling up may be pursued in relative safety. By contrast, the start-big method puts a large initial investment at risk. Even if it succeeds, it cannot be scaled up—proportionally—in the way innovations with smaller beginnings can. The result is a lower aggregate ROI. However, the small-beginnings strategy requires the cultural predisposition to rapidly scale up a business once considered minor when the large opportunity becomes clear.

Of course, there are exceptions to this pattern. You cannot invest incrementally in the next generation of a state-of-the-art microchip or a major-market automobile. But even these giant projects will go better if managers have been trained and qualified in a series of smaller intrapreneurial adventures.

How do you protect funds for smaller intrapreneurial projects when there is pressure to put all the eggs in a few giant baskets?

SOLUTIONS

A. Decide that innovation is everyone's job and that every business and every function is expected to innovate on a scale appropriate to its size.

B. Hold every business unit responsible for producing innovation in areas within and adjacent to their charter. Being smaller than the whole company, business units will fund smaller enterprises. Reward business unit leaders if they create a new business outside their charter, even if the new business has to be moved to another part of the organization. This will release innovation funding from many different sources. Business unit leaders will know that, come review time, they will be asked, "What innovations are coming out of your area? What successes have you funded?" (See "Measurement of innovation" on page 136.)

C. Provide resources to fund innovation at the lower levels of the organization. (See "Decision making by the doers" on page 124.)

STRETCH SOLUTIONS

A. Build an organization that can manage complexity. Develop the capacity to market many smaller products and services without creating confusion either within the organization or among your customers.

B. Foster many internal intraprises. These will serve as training and proving grounds for intrapreneurial talent and will help the organization to orient itself toward complexity.

CHOOSING WHICH INNOVATION SUCCESS FACTORS TO ADDRESS

We have now examined how each of the nineteen Innovation Success Factors can be strengthened. But how do you choose which factors to work on first? One method is suggested here.

After completing the Innovation Climate Questionnaire, look at your results. Plot each of the Innovation Success Factors on the matrix below, rating each factor on the following two scales:

1. *Current strength of the factor.* If the factor is already very strong in your organization, give it an A; if very weak, give it an F. For intermediate ranges, use B, C, and D.

	A					
Current	B					
strength	C					
of	D					
factor	F					
		A	B	C	D	F

Ease of strengthening factor

Success Factor Improvement Matrix

2. *Ease of strengthening the factor.* If a number of the suggested solutions look as though they would be effective, and if they would be easy to implement, give the factor an A. If none of the solutions look promising or if they would be virtually impossible to implement, give the factor an F. Again, B, C, and D cover points between.

Get together with others in the organization to discuss the results.

◾ Are you lucky? Are any factors rated both currently weak and easy to change? If so, go fix them! Check out the solutions suggested above.

◾ Look for factors that have only moderate strength and are pretty easy to change. Addressing a few of those quickly will build morale and draw other people into the change process.

◾ After that, choose a couple of weak factors that are a bit harder to change but have great value to the organization. Discuss in your group how they might be tackled.

ONE LAST RESOURCE

Link to the chat room called the Intrapreneurs' Café from www.intrapreneur.com and find people in other organizations who are improving their climate for innovation.

Chapter 14

The Future of the Intrapreneurial Organization

THE PROJECT-BASED ORGANIZATION of the future has a structure quite different from that of its predecessors. The line organization is relatively small. The majority of employees are knowledge workers, moving from project to project to meet the demands of the skeletal line organization, which focuses on bringing together all the forces needed to achieve its strategic intent. The knowledge workers are no longer subordinates to an unchanging boss but suppliers of intellectual services in a free internal market. The formal structure looks much like that of a "virtual" organization, which is a small line organization that contracts out most of the work to external suppliers. In the case of the intrapreneurial organization, many of the suppliers are teams of internal intrapreneurs, still employees of the organization both legally and in their sense of belonging.

INFORMATION
ENGINEERING ASSOCIATES

Early in the era of AIDS, the New York Blood Bank asked DuPont's Medical Products Department for help. DuPont sold the blood bank equipment to test for HIV in blood, but that was not enough. When HIV was found in a pint of blood, it had to be traced back to its source. This required a massive database that could track every pint of blood as it moved through the system from collection to transfusion. The blood bank needed such a database developed in ninety days.

The Medical Products Department sold blood analyzers, not computer software. But the blood bank was a good customer and desperate to prevent needless HIV infections. The department sought help both from its own information technology people and from the corporate staff. Neither could deliver within the ninety-day window.

By the standards of bureaucracy, the medical products account executive had done all he could for his customer. But he had heard of a very special intrapreneurial information technology group within DuPont's huge Fibers Department.

DuPont made fibers like nylon and Kevlar® for textiles, carpets, and industrial products like tire cords. Within the Fibers Department, Information Engineering Associates (IEA) had recently been formed to exploit CASE tools, a new technology for writing software faster. IEA had previously solved a problem very similar to that of the New York Blood Bank: the group had built a database to track the history and quality of every bobbin of Kevlar® fiber as it moved through the manufacturing plant in Richmond, Virginia.

Within traditional bureaucracy, a staff group from one division is not supposed to do major jobs for other divisions. But this was an emergency, so IEA got the job. It delivered the blood tracking database within the ninety-day deadline, and the Medical Products Department delivered a service that far exceeded a major customer's expectations. Breaking the rules of bureaucracy saved lives. Medical products got better service because it had a greater choice of internal vendors.

As IEA's reputation spread throughout DuPont, the group found itself creating a database to track radiation in the ground water in the test wells around DuPont's nuclear materials production site at Savannah River, Georgia. When it again succeeded in ninety days, groups all over DuPont wanted IEA's services.

Soon IEA's success began to be a problem. While the Fibers Department was paying the group's salaries, other departments were using its services, and the management of Fibers began to complain. IEA went to corporate finance and said,

"We are tired of being a staff group, we want to be an intrapreneurial profit center." The finance officer sighed. "A staff group becoming a profit center? Are you kidding?" Then he paused, and with a twinkle in his eye, said, "How would you like to be a negative cost center?" Of course, a "negative cost center" is essentially the same thing as a profit center, but the words suggest something different. This illustrates an important aspect of the corporate immune system: it responds to the outside of an idea—the words—not the true essence. When you run into a hyperactive immune system, change the words and keep going.

IEA went from being a staff group supposedly serving only Fibers to being an intraprise with clients throughout DuPont. This oasis of free intraprise resulted in new and better information technology service for every division of the company. Free intraprise provides a powerful mechanism for spreading learning across organizational boundaries.

While other information technology groups at DuPont were downsizing, IEA grew to 120 employees. The new technology spread rapidly across organizational boundaries. Serious safety problems were brought under control; lives were saved, and customers amazed. In this case as in many others, free intraprise greatly improved the efficiency of knowledge work by replacing bureaucracy with customer choice and supplier intrapreneurship.

In the organization of the future, free intraprise will be widespread. James Brian Quinn points out that virtually all employee activities can be seen as services provided to others within the firm.[10] Most of these services will be better provided by intraprises than by employees hampered by traditional chain-of-command controls. The bulk of employees will therefore be intrapreneurs operating internal service intraprises.

The intrapreneurial service-providers will not be out of control. Rather, they will be guided by "an invisible hand" to serve the needs articulated and funded by the line organization as it pursues the organizational mission and provides customer satisfaction at a profit.

In this new environment, employees will be both freer and more responsible. On the one hand, intrapreneurs will need to be given rights comparable to those of an entrepreneurial service provider (see Appendix F: The Intrapreneurial Bill of Rights). On the other, they will inevitably become responsible for renewing their own ability to add value and knowledge to projects; if they do not, they will find it increasingly difficult to find work. Despite the fact that they are employees, they will be "in business" to deliver services to a multiplicity of potential customers and will be in competition with a host of other professionals with similar knowledge. The flexibility they enjoy will encourage the transfer of technology and learning across all organizational boundaries.

Intrapreneurial teams will continually develop new capabilities that will keep them valued and in demand in the future. They will spend their "profits" on training and productivity tools to achieve those ends. As a result, there will be many sharp thinkers distributed throughout the organization exploring and developing the core competencies that will produce future competitive advantages for the organization as a whole.

The result of a free intraprise structure will be the creation of an organization with great capacity for learning. Just as the brain learns by forming new connections among nerve cells, organizations learn by forming new relationships among individuals and teams. The fluid organizations of the future are self-organizing systems, with each individual and each team constantly seeking ways to become more valuable and to contribute more. The internal market provides much of the feedback that is needed to guide this self-directed activity toward the good of the organization and its external customers. (For more on this, see *The Intelligent Organization*.)

Hierarchical organizations develop an army of specialists but provide little experience that leads to general management skills. Consequently,, there is a great shortage of proven general managers. In the future, all intrapreneurial teams will learn business judgment by running their intraprises. From the very start of their careers, team members will be helping to manage small profit centers and learning from the experience of their teams' successes and failures. When the time comes to find general management talent for the line organization, many experienced and tested intrapreneurs will be available. By their records shall ye know them.

To our great satisfaction, one of the leaders in building this new type of organization is not a business corporation but a government agency. As described in Chapter 4, the U.S. Forest Service has taken bold steps to create a supportive environment for intrapreneurial knowledge workers. It has created a robust internal market economy.

We should not be surprised that a new pattern of work is evolving as we leave the industrial era and enter the information age. The new relationship between individuals and the organization is at once far freer and far more capable of bringing about order in a complex and rapidly changing marketplace. It is as different from the typical relationships of the industrial age as those are from the relationship between serf and lord.

In short, bureaucracy is no more appropriate to the information age than feudalism was to the industrial era. Let us give thanks for a new era of freedom, flexibility, challenge, and learning. Let us enjoy the rebirth of the sense of community that bureaucracy briefly destroyed.

APPENDICES

Appendices

If you would like to use any of the appendices, downloadable versions are available from www.pinchot.com.

Appendix A:
The Intrapreneur's
Ten Commandments

1. Remember, it is easier to ask for forgiveness than for permission.

2. Do any job needed to make your project work, regardless of your job description.

3. Come to work each day willing to be fired.

4. Recruit a strong team.

5. Ask for advice before resources.

6. Forget pride of authorship, spread credit widely.

7. When you bend the rules, keep the best interests of the company and its customers in mind.

8. Honor your sponsors.

9. Underpromise and overdeliver.

10. Be true to your goals, but realistic about ways to achieve them.

APPENDIX B:
AN OUTLINE FOR AN
INTRAPRENEURIAL BUSINESS PLAN

I. EXECUTIVE SUMMARY

An executive summary is generally written last. Don't worry about it yet. When done writing the rest of the plan, summarize the essence.

II. THE BUSINESS

Generally describe the business.

- What is the product or service?
- Who benefits from it and how does it make their lives better?
- Briefly, how is it superior to competing methods for satisfying the need?

    (This is a good place for your value proposition.)

III. THE MARKET

A. STRUCTURE AND SIZE OF THE TARGET MARKET

- Who are you trying to reach with this business?
- Why these customers?
- How many of them are there? (Make a wild guess.)
- Are their numbers growing or shrinking? Why?
- How can you identify them or reach them?

B. PICTURE OF CUSTOMERS AND THEIR NEEDS

- What is happening in the lives of this group of people?
- What need is unfulfilled?
- Why is this need growing (if it is)?
- How will your product or service fill that need?

Note: you may have several layers of customers—for example, those you sell to directly and *their* customers, who also use the functionality you create. Or there may be several distinct types of customers (segments). In those cases, describe the top two or three kinds, their needs, and how you address them.

IV. THE COMPETITION

A. CURRENT COMPETITORS

Make a chart of the direct competitors for this customer's business. Assess the strengths and weaknesses of each. How would you learn more about them?

COMPETITOR	STRENGTHS	WEAKNESSES	HOW YOU ARE BETTER

B. POTENTIAL COMPETITORS

What competition might arise in the next few years that doesn't exist today? Create a second chart for these competitors. How can you make your business strategy robust enough to deal with them?

COMPETITOR	STRENGTHS	WEAKNESSES	HOW YOU ARE BETTER

C. OTHER KINDS OF COMPETITION

- In what other ways might customers address the same needs (including doing nothing about them)?
- How else could they change their lives for the better in this area?
- How can you win customers' preferences relative to these other options?

V. THE MARKETING AND SALES PLAN

A. MARKET POSITION

- How do you want this business to be seen in the marketplace (expensive or cheap, wild or conservative, strong or flexible, etc.)?
- What can you do to get people to see you in the way you wish to be seen?

B. PRICING STRATEGY

- How would you charge—by the item? by the hour? by the experience? by the project? by the result?
- Give examples of your pricing, e.g., hourly or daily rates, price per item, typical project size and cost.
- How do your prices compare to those of your competitors?
- How do your prices relate to what customers will be willing to pay?
- How do they relate to your costs?

C. THE SALES CYCLE

1. MARKET AWARENESS PLAN

- How will customers become aware of your business?
- What will make them want your product or service?

2. Lead generation and screening

- How will you generate names of people to talk to about your business?
- How will you screen them for follow-up?

3. Selling and closing

- What medium will you use to convert interested leads to ready-to-buy customers—phone? mail? word of mouth?
- What is your opening sales pitch?
- What major objections do you anticipate, and how will you handle them?
- How will you close sales?
- What will be the clincher that gets customers to commit once their major objections are handled?

4. Post-sales support

- What do you plan to do to support customers after the sale?

VI. THE PRODUCT AND SERVICE DEVELOPMENT PLAN

- What has to be done to turn your product or service into something you can sell in quantity?
  - ⇨ Product design
  - ⇨ Production process
  - ⇨ Tools
  - ⇨ Staff hiring and training
- Describe projects, development milestones with dates, and very rough costs in effort and dollars to reach the milestones.

VII. DELIVERY PLAN

- How will you deliver your benefit to the customer once the business is up and running? Make a detailed list of the steps.
- Estimate the costs of delivery.
  - ⇨ Per unit
  - ⇨ Per month

VIII. THE VENTURE TEAM

- Who will work on this with you? Who will be the key founders?
- How will decisions be made?
- How will team members be compensated?
- How will new hires and outsiders be integrated into the team?

IX. PARTNERING STRATEGY

- Who might you partner with to give this business more reach?
- What would the role of each partner in the collaboration be?

X. SUMMARY OF RISKS AND ASSUMPTIONS

- What are the most likely ways in which this could go wrong?
- What would the consequences be?
- Are the consequences of failure bearable?
- What are the assumptions to test?

XI. THE FINANCIAL GUESTIMATES

Give a several-year summary of your wild guesses as to business costs and revenue. Use a spreadsheet like the one on the next page.

Projected Income Statement

	YEAR 1	YEAR 2	YEAR 3	YEAR 4	YEAR 5
A. Sales					
Cost of sales					
B. Variable labor					
C. Variable materials & services					
D. **Direct variable expenses (B+C)**					
E. **Gross profit**					
Operating expenses					
F. Team salaries & fringes					
G. Allocated overheads					
H. Rent, utilities, etc.					
I. Marketing & sales					
J. R&D, quality					
K. Training					
L. Depreciation					
M. Other					
N. **Total operating expenses**					
O. **Earnings from operations (A-(D+N))**					
P. **Cost of capital**					
Q. **Net income (loss) (N-O)**					

APPENDIX C:
THE INTRAPRENEURIAL
EVALUATION CHECKLIST

When making an investment decision about an intrapreneurial investment, use this checklist to be sure you have a strong intrapreneur. Remember: bet on people, not just ideas, so give close attention to checking out intrapreneurs as individuals and as a team. Below are a number of characteristics of successful intrapreneurs. To what extent does the intrapreneur you are examining display each of them relative to the general population of employees?

A: To an exceptional degree   **B**: More than most
C: About average   **D**: Below average

	A	B	C	D
Has clear vision of "how" as well as of the final objective	❏	❏	❏	❏
Already in action—doesn't expect you to wave a wand and do it all	❏	❏	❏	❏
Is a moderate risk taker; is optimistic, but not out of touch with reality	❏	❏	❏	❏
Has "fire in the belly"— cares about the idea	❏	❏	❏	❏
Sees the barriers clearly and plans ways to circumvent them	❏	❏	❏	❏
Has used whatever freedom has been available to act innovatively	❏	❏	❏	❏
Has inspired others to help, even when they were not assigned	❏	❏	❏	❏

	A	B	C	D
Has been trustworthy and honest	❏	❏	❏	❏
Even when breaking the rules, works in the best interests of the company and its customers	❏	❏	❏	❏

APPENDIX D:
THE SPONSOR
EVALUATION CHECKLIST

Below are a number of characteristics of successful sponsors. To what extent does the candidate display each of them relative to the general population of managers?

A: To an exceptional degree   **B**: More than most
C: About average   **D**: Below average

	A	B	C	D
Passes the company vision on in an inspiring way	❑	❑	❑	❑
Good at selecting the right intrapreneurs to trust	❑	❑	❑	❑
Helps build good cross-functional teams	❑	❑	❑	❑
Good at getting resources and permissions for the team	❑	❑	❑	❑
Asks tough questions without taking over the team	❑	❑	❑	❑
Shelters his or her people when they make "original" mistakes	❑	❑	❑	❑
Helps intrapreneurs avoid political pitfalls	❑	❑	❑	❑
Helps establish achievable milestones	❑	❑	❑	❑

	A	B	C	D
Draws others in as joint sponsors	❑	❑	❑	❑
Sees that the team stays with the project and gets proper recognition	❑	❑	❑	❑
Has a good five-year average in risk taking	❑	❑	❑	❑

APPENDIX E:
THE TEAM EFFECTIVENESS
CHECKLIST

Take a reading on team effectiveness every week or so by having each team member rate the team's performance on the factors below. Use the following grades:

A: This is a major team strength   **B**: We are doing quite well on this
C: So so—needs improvement   **D**: Weakness in this area is serious

	DATE:	DATE:	DATE:	DATE:	DATE:
Clearly defined outcomes					
Continuity of relationship					
Inspiring common purposes					
Measurable goals and deadlines					
Agreement on how and when					
A common fate (all go up and down together)					
Competent and committed team members					
Good communication, quick feedback, open information					
A strong network with other teams, intraprises, and enterprises					
Mutual support					

APPENDIX F:
THE INTRAPRENEURIAL
BILL OF RIGHTS

1. *The 10 percent rule:* An employee may use 10 percent of her time to pursue new ideas she believes may be useful to the organization.

2. *The right to form an intraprise:* An employee has the right to form an intraprise if his salary can be covered by revenue from customers or intracapital.

3. *The right to one's intraprise:* An intrapreneurial team that has created a profitable or solvent business has a quasi-ownership right to continue operating it. It cannot be taken and given to others without cause and due process.

4. *The right to join an intraprise:* Every employee has the right to join an intraprise, provided the intraprise is agreeable and is able and willing to pay her salary.

5. *The right to reject team members:* Every intraprise has the right not to accept members it considers unsuitable, and to ask members to leave according to a process designated in the team bylaws. No outside entity can force a team to keep a member it has asked to leave. The larger organization will provide a safety net for employees leaving intrapreneurial teams.

6. *The right to save:* The team, or an individual intrapreneur, has the right to deposit receipts in the intracapital bank, where they cannot be appropriated by any other entity except as the result of due process or corporate taxation at normal rates.

7. *The right of possession:* When an intraprise buys tools or other business assets with its own intracapital, it has a quasi-ownership right to control the use and disposition of those assets for the furtherance of its work.

8. *The right to spend:* Intrapreneurs and intraprises have the right to spend their intracapital as they see fit for any legitimate intraprise or corporate purpose. They may not use it for personal expenditures unrelated to the business unless it is first paid to them as personal compensation in a program approved by human resources.

9. *The right to lead:* The leader of an intrapreneurial team shall not be removed from that position as long as he or she has the support of the team.

10. *Freedom of speech:* Intrapreneurs have the right to speak freely on all matters concerning the governance of the organization.

THE INTRAPRENEURIAL UNDERGROUND

Help us build the intrapreneurial underground. The underground exists to transport intrapreneurial talent from organizations that mistreat and misuse intrapreneurs to organizations that better appreciate their intentions, style, and talents.

Do you

- Need to recruit one or more intrapreneurs?
- Need to find a company that appreciates intrapreneurs?
- Need some comradeship and supportive dialogue with other intrapreneurs?

If so, check out the Intrapreneurs' Café link from www.intrapreneur.com and compare experiences with people from other firms. And if you wish, help us build a website that services the world's intrapreneurs.

Notes

1. Peter F. Drucker, *Management Challenges for the 21st Century* (New York: Harperbusiness, 1999), 119.

2. Gifford Pinchot, *Intrapreneuring: Why You Don't Have to Leave the Corporation to Become an Entrapreneur* (San Francisco: Berrett-Koehler, 1999).

3. Gifford Pinchot and Elizabeth Pinchot, *The Intelligent Organization* (San Francisco: Berrett-Koehler, 1994).

4. William van Dusen Wishard, "The American Future," *World Business Academy Perspectives* 6, no. 3 (1992): 35.

5. Elliott Jaques, *A General Theory of Bureaucracy* (New York: Wiley, 1976).

6. Frances Hesselbein, Marshall Goldsmith, Richard Beckhard, and Richard F. Schubert, eds., *The Community of the Future* (Drucker Foundation Future Series) (San Francisco: Jossey-Bass, 1998).

7. Lewis Hyde, *The Gift: Imagination and the Erotic Life of Property* (New York: Vintage, 1979).

8. Jack Stack and Bo Burlingham, *The Great Game of Business* (New York: Doubleday, 1992).

9. John Schuster, Jill Carpenter with M. Patricia Kane, *The Power of Open-Book Management: Releasing the Potential of People's Minds, Hearts, and Hands* (New York: Wiley, 1996).

10. James Brian Quinn, *Intelligent Enterprise: A Knowledge and Service Based Paradigm for Industry* (New York: Free Press, 1992), 41.

Index

About the Authors

Gifford Pinchot is a leading teacher, consultant, author, and speaker on innovation management. He has helped launch more than four hundred ventures, consulted for over half the Fortune 100 companies, licensed two of his patents, and discussed his work on *Larry King Live* and *The Today Show.* His firm, Pinchot & Company, helps large corporations overcome bureaucratic obstacles to change, renewal, employee empowerment, and environmental innovation.

As a CEO, Mr. Pinchot has also built and sold three other firms—in manufacturing, in services, and in Internet security software.

Pinchot graduated from Harvard in 1965 with an A.B. degree with honors in economics and subsequently studied sociology and neurophysiology at Johns Hopkins University.

He is the author of two previous books and numerous articles. *Intrapreneuring: Why You Don't Have to Leave the Corporation to Become an Entrepreneur* (Harper & Row, 1985; reissued by Berrett-Koehler, 1999) defined the ground rules for the courageous pursuit of new ideas in established organizations. The book has been published in fifteen languages, and the word *intrapreneuring,* coined by Pinchot, is now recognized by major dictionaries, including the *American Heritage Dictionary* and *The Oxford Dictionary of the English Language.*

The Intelligent Organization (Berrett-Koehler, 1994), written with Elizabeth Pinchot, described, among other things, a revolutionary way of organizing every kind of work, from the most innovative to the most mundane.

Business consultant **Ron Pellman** is head of Pellman EnterpriZes, Inc., as well as a member of the Pinchot & Company network, and an associate of New Business Search & Development International Corp. He learned how innovation works from his own intrapreneurial successes and failures and by helping prominent companies in the U.S. and Europe on over three hundred new product, new business development, and technology planning projects. He has directed numerous seminars on creative problem solving, new product development, and innovation management.

Pellman majored in fine arts at the University of Buffalo and in 1963 received a B.S. in mechanical engineering from Carnegie Mellon. He has also done postgraduate work in electronics.

In the 1960s, he was principal engineer at the Ford Motor Company's Advanced Vehicle Concepts Department, where he was first exposed to the application of creative techniques to product development and business innovation.

His subsequent consulting career included a founding partnership in a company that specialized in innovative solutions to business growth problems and the U.S. divisional presidency of an international firm whose dual focus was technical problem solving and new product development services.

For eight years, Pellman was president of Pinchot & Company, where he helped both large and small organizations rekindle their intrapreneurial spirit.

As an inventor, he has secured patents ranging from a novel transmission shift system to a new type of frozen food cutter. He is also a husband, father, grandfather, artist/craftsman, and former race car designer and driver.

Berrett–Koehler
Publishers

Berrett-Koehler is an independent publisher dedicated to an ambitious mission: *Creating a World That Works for All*.

We believe that to truly create a better world, action is needed at all levels—individual, organizational, and societal. At the individual level, our publications help people align their lives with their values and with their aspirations for a better world. At the organizational level, our publications promote progressive leadership and management practices, socially responsible approaches to business, and humane and effective organizations. At the societal level, our publications advance social and economic justice, shared prosperity, sustainability, and new solutions to national and global issues.

A major theme of our publications is "Opening Up New Space." Berrett-Koehler titles challenge conventional thinking, introduce new ideas, and foster positive change. Their common quest is changing the underlying beliefs, mindsets, institutions, and structures that keep generating the same cycles of problems, no matter who our leaders are or what improvement programs we adopt.

We strive to practice what we preach—to operate our publishing company in line with the ideas in our books. At the core of our approach is stewardship, which we define as a deep sense of responsibility to administer the company for the benefit of all of our "stakeholder" groups: authors, customers, employees, investors, service providers, and the communities and environment around us.

We are grateful to the thousands of readers, authors, and other friends of the company who consider themselves to be part of the "BK Community." We hope that you, too, will join us in our mission.

A BK Business Book

This book is part of our BK Business series. BK Business titles pioneer new and progressive leadership and management practices in all types of public, private, and nonprofit organizations. They promote socially responsible approaches to business, innovative organizational change methods, and more humane and effective organizations.

Berrett–Koehler
Publishers

A community dedicated to creating
a world that works for all

Visit Our Website: www.bkconnection.com

Read book excerpts, see author videos and Internet movies, read our
authors' blogs, join discussion groups, download book apps, find out about
the BK Affiliate Network, browse subject-area libraries of books, get special
discounts, and more!

Subscribe to Our Free E-Newsletter, the *BK Communiqué*

Be the first to hear about new publications, special discount offers, exclusive articles, news about bestsellers, and more! Get on the list for our free
e-newsletter by going to **www.bkconnection.com**.

Get Quantity Discounts

Berrett-Koehler books are available at quantity discounts for orders of ten or
more copies. Please call us toll-free at (800) 929-2929 or email us at **bkp
.orders@aidcvt.com**.

Join the BK Community

BKcommunity.com is a virtual meeting place where people from around
the world can engage with kindred spirits to create a world that works for
all. **BKcommunity.com** members may create their own profiles, blog, start
and participate in forums and discussion groups, post photos and videos,
answer surveys, announce and register for upcoming events, and chat with
others online in real time. Please join the conversation!